GOD'S MOUNTAIN MAN

The Story of Jedediah Strong Smith

ESTHER LOEWEN VOGT

Gospel Publishing House
Springfield, Missouri
02–0563

To Gordon Adams, my son-in-law
A man of courage and determination
Who too set foot in Oregon country

Library of Congress Cataloging-in-Publication Data

Vogt, Esther Loewen.
  God's mountain man : the story of Jedediah Strong Smith / Esther Loewen Vogt.
     p. cm.
  Includes bibliographical references.
  Summary: Follows the life of the nineteenth-century trapper and explorer who earned his reputation on the western frontier.
  ISBN 0–88243–563–9 (paperback)
  1. Smith, Jedediah Strong, 1799–1831—Juvenile literature. 2. Explorers—West (U.S.)—Biography—Juvenile literature. 3. Fur traders—West (U.S.)—Biography—Junvenile literature. 4. Trappers—West (U.S.)—Biography—Juvenile literature 5. West (U.S.)—Description and travel—To 1848—Juvenile literature. [1. Smith, Jedediah Strong, 1799–1831. 2. Explorers.] I. Title.
F592.S649V64 1991
978'.02'092—dc20
[B]
[92]   90–25278

Printed in the United States of America

"Yet was he modest, never obtrusive, charitable ... a man whom none could approach without respect, or know without esteem. And though he fell under the spear ... and none can tell where his bones are bleaching, he must not be forgotten" (*Jedediah Strong Smith,* an anonymous eulogy in *Illinois Monthly Magazine,* 1832).

Table of Contents

Foreword   7

Author's Note   9

Map: Jed's Journeys West of the Rocky
        Mountains   10

Map: Jed's Journeys East of the Rocky Mountains   11

1. Young Tracker   13
2. A Special Gift   19
3. A Hard Hunting Lesson   23
4. Adventures on the Great Lakes   27
5. Down the Ohio and up the Mississippi   32
6. Trouble on the Missouri   41
7. "Watch out for the Rees!"   47
8. Learning to Trap   51
9. A Battle with the Rees   57
10. "I'll Go"   63
11. Grizzly Attack   68
12. Learning an Indian Secret   75
13. A Surprise among the Flatheads   82
14. Beyond the Shining Mountains   86

15. "I Am Not a Spy!"   94
16. Death Stalks the Desert   99
17. Keeping a Promise   107
18. More Trouble with the Governor   114
19. Up the Wild Coast   120
20. Massacre   126
21. White-headed Eagle   131
22. Wintering at Ft. Vancouver   137
23. Thoughts of Home   142
24. Good-bye, Shining Mountains   147
25. Jed's Last Adventure   153
For Further Reading   160

Foreword

In the hearts of most boys is reserved a warm spot for the American mountain man. He is often perceived as a kind of John Wayne—one that you and I might desire as our hero. Somewhere in this image we have painted him as a rough but God-fearing man. He's not necessarily gentle, but the kind of guy one would take a liking to.

Not so. The common mountain man was whisky-drinkin', knife-totin', and far from being a Christian. The best place for such a godless man to live was the mountains—far, far away from other human beings.

But Jedediah Smith was different. Here, as presented from the pages of history by Esther L. Vogt, is a person who walked and talked with the Almighty Creator. It was at an early age Jedediah asked Jesus Christ into his heart. From that point forward, life's adventure began. With his plunder bag, holding his most precious Bible, Jedediah blazed a trail westward. In spite of the dangers and obstacles of life, or maybe because of them, Jedediah took the time to read the precious Word and to ask God for daily guidance.

A special friend in Jedediah's life was Dr. Titus Simons. During those formative years the doctor was there nurturing young Jedediah and encouraging him in the reading of God's Word. All through life Jedediah continued to think fondly of Dr. Simons—the one who had invested in him. Such a relationship is unique to that special one developed between a Royal Rangers commander and his boys.

Among mountain men Jedediah Smith stands tall, especially spiritually speaking. For he was God's mountain man, described by the author as one "in whose blood surged the spirit of adventure, but whose soul trusted the living God." Furthermore, Jedediah demonstrated (without realizing it of course) unswerving obedience to the Royal Rangers Motto: Ready.

If given the opportunity, most Royal Rangers would have welcomed Jedediah into the Trailblazer outpost. A Trailblazer is one who goes into new lands and places to blaze a trail for others to follow. The adventuresome Trailblazer possesses high character and a deep faith in God. Yes, Jedediah would have fit in.

KEN HUNT
NATIONAL COMMANDER
ROYAL RANGERS

8

Author's Note

My main goal in writing this book has been to show the reader that Jedediah Strong Smith was an adventurer who experienced the leading and protection of God. Every attempt has been made to present accurate information. However, some sources differ in their accounts of the events of Jedediah's life. Where accounts varied, the one thought to be most accurate was used.

JED'S JOURNEYS WEST OF THE ROCKY MOUNTAINS

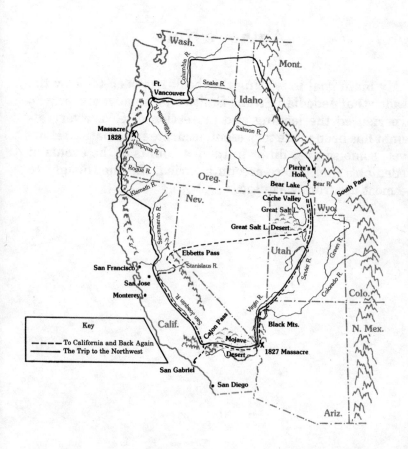

JED'S JOURNEYS EAST OF THE ROCKY MOUNTAINS

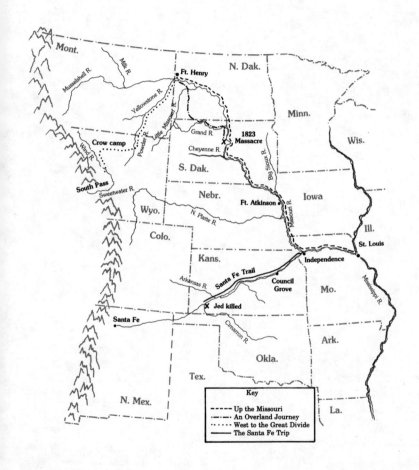

1
Young Tracker

Dry leaves crunched underfoot as Jedediah Smith and Toby Warner walked in silence through the Pennsylvania woods, not far from Lake Erie, one warm autumn afternoon in the year of 1810.

Jed raised his blue eyes toward the sky. "Time's a-wasting, Toby," he said. "We'd better hustle if we're to get back before dark. How far is it to your uncle's cabin?"

"Oh, I dunno." Toby paused and shifted his parcel of butter to the other hand. "He lives down this path a-ways. We should reach the clearin' after a bit. What's your hurry, Jed?"

"I promised Dr. Simons I'd stop by his place. He's got something to show me. Why don't we take a shortcut? Your butter will be fresher that way."

Toby sighed. "Well, I sure don't want to get lost. Besides, I don't know any shortcuts."

"Neither do I. But a body can always learn." Jed grinned, then added, "I'm twelve years old and getting older. There's so much to know. How will I ever learn it all?"

He paused and peered among the trees. "Let's go that way. I think we'll reach the clearing quicker if we do."

Without another word Jed turned from the path and skirted the heavy underbrush around the trees. He heard Toby grunting behind him.

After walking for a few minutes, Jed stopped. "Looks like Indians have been through this part lately."

"Indians!" Toby gasped. "How do you know!"

"Look right over there. See that nick on the tree trunk? It means 'Here is the trail.' And there's a broken twig left hanging. See? Another Indian sign." Jed knelt on the ground and pointed to the twig: "It means 'This is the trail.'"

"Shouldn't we—uh, g-go back on the p-path?" Toby sputtered. "If we meet—"

"There's nothing to be afraid of, Toby," said Jed, rising. "These signs are at least three days old. See how the twig fails to spring back when I touch it?"

"Do you think we'll reach my Uncle Joe's place soon?" asked Toby, looking first over one shoulder and then the other.

Jed walked on without speaking until they reached a clearing. Suddenly he pointed. "Look. Is that your uncle's cabin?"

Toby let out his breath slowly. "Sure is." He turned to Jed. "I guess what the other boys say must be true. You *are* an Indian tracker!"

Jed's neck reddened some but he was pleased.

The door to the log cabin in the middle of the clearing stood open. A wiry brown and tan dog bounded out with a welcome bark, and a lanky, middle-aged man with steely gray eyes and a shaggy brown beard followed.

"Well, well, Toby!" the man said. "I see you're here with my weekly ration of fresh butter. I don't know what I'd do without it. But I didn't expect you so soon."

"My friend Jedediah Smith here decided on a shortcut. He says Indians have been around these woods lately. See any, Uncle Joe?"

The man squatted down on the small porch made of rough-hewn boards and motioned the boys to sit beside him. He shrugged his blue-shirted shoulders.

"Oh, they were friendly Delawares, and that was a few days ago. I gave them some cornbread, the last of my butter, and some rabbit stew, and they left. But some war-like tribes are sneakin' around this territory, so it pays to be

14

careful. Tell me, Jed, how'd you know Indians were through here? And how'd you keep from gettin' lost in these woods?"

Jed reddened again and he coughed. "I just try to notice everything my eyes see."

"Boys in Erie call Jed an Indian tracker," Toby put in. "Jed's always explorin' the woods and streams."

"How come you do that, boy?" Uncle Joe asked. "Are you from Pennsylvania?"

A deer bounded across the far end of the clearing into the deep woods as Jed took a breath to answer. "No, sir. We moved here from New York. My father owned a store where he traded with trappers and Indians. My great grandfather (on my mother's side) was an Indian fighter. He was killed fighting Indians. I was named for him, Jedediah Strong. So I guess I come by all this kind of natural."

"Hmmm. Maybe someday you'll go adventurin' yourself, Jed," Uncle Joe said, thoughtfully stroking his beard.

"I sure hope so. Sometimes it's hard to wait until I grow up." Jed stood up and brushed the dirt from the seat of his brown homespun trousers. "I think we'd better go, Toby, if we're to stop at Dr. Simons'."

After a drink of fresh cold water from the spring behind the cabin, the two boys made their way through the woods, following the shortcut they had taken on the way down.

Once out of the woods, they followed the narrow dirt road that followed the bend of the river. Up ahead, Dr. Titus Simons' log house sat like a speckled brown and white bird in its green nest of trees and wild plum bushes. The doctor was both physician and teacher, and the Smith and Simons families were best friends. The doctor was often visiting sick people in the area, but when he was home he always welcomed young Jed Smith.

"Jed, I gotta go home and help my father with evening chores."

Jed nodded and watched for a moment, until Toby, picking up his pace, rounded a bend in the trail and was out of sight. Jed walked up the path to the cabin alone. When he

15

knocked, the door opened and in the doorway stood his friend, the tall, lean doctor.

"Come in, my boy," Dr. Simons said. "I've got something I know will interest you." He motioned Jed to a chair beside the square, homemade wooden table.

"What is it, Dr. Simons?" Jed sat on the edge of the seat leaning forward with his hands on his knees.

"It's a journal about Lewis and Clark and their expedition to the Northwest, written by Patrick Goss, who went with them."

Waves of excitement coursed down Jed's spine. "Could I see it, please? I'm itching to go West myself."

"Yes, I know, Jed. And that dream will be closer when we all move over into Ohio." The doctor spoke of plans that had been brewing in the Simons and Smith families ever since Indian troubles, despite the fort, began breaking out around the settlement of Erie.

Jed leafed through the journal that told how Meriweather Lewis and William Clark, with a party of explorers, had made an expedition to the Columbia River (in what is now Washington State) in 1804 and returned in 1806. Excitement pounded in Jed's veins. *Why, that was just a few years ago!* Jed thought. Much still remained to be explored. *Someday,* he promised himself, *someday I'll set foot in the western wilderness myself!*

Finally Jed reluctantly closed the book. "I've got to go."

"Well, take it with you; look at it some more; show it to your family!" said Dr. Simons, chuckling.

When Jed neared home, the fragrance of venison stew bubbling in the outdoor cooking pot and cornbread baking on the open earth drifted to his nostrils. This cabin had been Jed's home since he was nine and the family had moved to Erie, Pennsylvania.

Jedediah Strong Smith had been born to Jedediah and Sally Smith on Sunday, June 24, 1798, in Bainbridge, New York, in Chenango County. His father operated a trading post on the banks of the Susquehannah River but felt the urge to move on. In Erie, Pennsylvania, Jed's love for ad-

16

venture grew, and he spent many hours exploring the woods and streams and along the banks of Lake Erie itself. He also learned all he could about Indian signs.

"Hey, Wampum!"

A big brown dog with a graying muzzle lumbered out to meet Jed. His mother was just spreading the table with a fresh white cloth when Jed came in.

She paused, her tall pregnant figure leaning against the table. Her hair wound into a tight bun on the nape of her neck was the same shade of brown as Jed's.

"You're later than I expected, Jed," she said. "But that was thoughtful of you to ask Toby to tell me you were visiting Dr. Simons. But don't you think you'd better get busy with your Bible verses?"

"Yes, ma'am."

Jed laid the journal down and picked up the heavy family Bible lying beside the clock that ticked on the wall shelf. He sat down in the open doorway of the cabin where the light was better and flipped the well-worn pages with their many underlined verses. Each time Jed learned another verse he underlined it. But his mind wasn't on the verses today. After all, he had read the Bible through just this past year. He couldn't help thinking of the family move to Ohio in a few weeks.

"Jed," his mother called, "can you recite Romans 8:18?"

"Wh—? Oh, yes, ma'am. I think so. 'For I reckon that the sufferings of this present time are not worthy to be compared with the glory which shall be revealed in us.' It's hard to concentrate on memorizing when I know we'll soon be moving West. I can scarcely wait."

His mother laughed. "Jedediah Strong Smith! You're absolutely a true Strong. I can see it bustin' out all over you, so I guess you can't help the blood of adventure running in your veins." Then growing thoughtful, she added, "You realize, young man, that you could actually be going out to meet suffering that way, don't you? . . . Well, it's still half an hour until supper. Why don't you practice shooting until

17

I call you? A good frontiersman must know how to shoot a gun."

Jed sprang to his feet. *"Yes, ma'am!"* He rushed into the cabin, replaced the Bible on its shelf, and picked up his gun from above the stone fireplace.

Mother was right. Adventure ran in his blood. Sometimes he felt it *sang* in his veins.

2

A Special Gift

The move by covered wagon in 1811 to Ashtabula, Ohio—
though little more than twenty miles west and still very
near Lake Erie—was a step closer to Jed's dream. Ashtabula
was a new settlement, having been located on the Ashtabula
River only eight years earlier. The Smith and Simons families built their cabins near each other. For days the ring
of axes and smell of freshly cut logs filled the air. The cabin
was up just in time for brother Austin to be born in it.

Although thirteen-year-old Jed helped his father with the
work, there was also time for fun. Dr. Simons' son Solomon
and daughter Louisa joined Jed and his brother, Ralph, and
sisters, Eunice, Sally, and Betsy in their games. The children explored the nearby woods and gathered pecans in the
groves. Sometimes they floated down the river on a homemade raft. They all loved the outdoors.

One day as the raft drifted lazily down the muddy river,
Jed's blue eyes stared off into the distance.

"Jed's probably in some wild, unknown world again," Solomon joshed, and the others laughed.

Jed looked up startled, and laughed too. "Oh, I guess I
am."

"Remember the time we got to Erie on that heavy flatboat
and you were so excited?" Ralph recalled. "You were sure
all sorts of wild adventures were waiting. In fact, you were
ready to take on Indians and kill bears the minute we
landed!"

"Well, I was only nine," Jed said sheepishly.

Betsy tucked her blue figured calico skirt over her bare knees. "Yes, and remember the song we made up? 'Jed Smith, the Indian fighter; Jed Smith, the great bear man'!" She laughed.

Jed grinned, remembering. Pennsylvania hadn't been too exciting, with more settlers moving in. But here was a new frontier. Someday his chance for adventure would come.

By this time there were eleven children in the Smith family, and Sally Strong Smith decided that Ashtabula was where they would stay.

"Jedediah," she announced to her husband one evening, "no more moving around. I want our children to grow up here, attend church, and go to school."

Although there was no school near Ashtabula, Dr. Simons taught the children in the community, as well as cared for the sick. He was especially fond of young Jed Smith.

Often when the doctor came home late at night, worn out from a long trip to see a patient, Jed would be waiting for him. The boy's eagerness to learn arithmetic, English, Bible, and history made Dr. Simons forget how tired he was.

One evening Jed was bubbling with excitement. "That journal about Lewis and Clark got me to thinking, Doctor. How did we get all that country they crossed—the Louisiana Territory?"

"I'm glad you asked, Jed," Dr. Simons said. "The Louisiana Territory stretches west from the Mississippi River to the Rocky Mountains. On the South is the Gulf of Mexico, and Canada is to the north. It takes in the important part of New Orleans at the mouth of the Mississippi. For a long time Spain owned the Louisiana Territory. But in 1800 Napoleon of France forced Spain to give it to France."

He paused, then went on. "Americans who lived along the Mississippi and Ohio rivers grew worried. Farmers floated their crops down the Mississippi and sold them in New Orleans. The farmers were afraid France wouldn't let Americans trade in that city. People who lived in Ohio, Kentucky, and Tennessee wanted to go to war to take New

Orleans from France, but President Thomas Jefferson didn't want war. Still, he thought New Orleans should belong to the United States. So he sent his friend James Monroe to France to see if they could buy it from Napoleon."

"And did they?"

The doctor nodded. "Napoleon really surprised them. He swept his hand over the map and offered to sell the entire Louisiana Territory to the United States."

"But why did he do that? If he had kept all that land . . ."

"Well, Napoleon was getting ready to fight England again," said Dr. Simons. "He knew the British navy could keep France from sending soldiers to New Orleans. This meant France might lose the territory to England. Why not make some money by selling the whole territory to the United States? His price was $15 million. This pushed the American frontier fifteen hundred miles farther west. Now the Mississippi would be a safe waterway for farmers and merchants."

"So that's how we got that wild mountain country."

"If you ask me, it's one of the greatest land bargains in the world. Yes, it may be wild with animals and mountains and Indians, but I believe someday it will be a rich land of farms and cities."

The Louisiana Purchase had more than doubled the territory of the United States. It contained areas which were later to become Louisiana, Arkansas, Oklahoma, Missouri, Kansas, Nebraska, Iowa, North Dakota, South Dakota, Montana, Minnesota, Colorado, and Wyoming.

"If only I could explore it someday!" Jed exclaimed. "Why did Lewis and Clark travel over the territory? Did they have adventurin' in their blood too?"

"Perhaps so. In any event, President Jefferson wanted to open this new territory to settlers; yet little was known about it. So he ordered Meriweather Lewis and William Clark to explore it. They were to make maps of the Missouri River and the Rocky Mountains and to describe what they saw. That's what's in the journal you read. They started in the spring of 1804 and came back in the fall of 1806. They went northwest, up the Missouri River, and crossed the Rocky Mountains, then along the Columbia River clear to the Pacific Ocean."

"Yes, that's what the journal said."

"Here, let me show you on the map I have. See, here's the Allegheny River, and there's Pittsburgh, and there's Ohio, and that's St. Louis." The two pored over the map for some time, then Jed looked up.

"But what of the country *south* of the Columbia River? Is there another way to cross the Rocky Mountains and go to the Southwest? It seems there are lots of white spaces on the map in that direction. Wouldn't I like to fill in those white spaces!" Jed's eyes shone.

The doctor laughed. "Well, Spain may have something to say about that. But, who knows, perhaps by the time you're older, we'll own that part of the country too. Right now you must study hard and prepare yourself. So let's turn to the Bible. Remember, Jed, no man will go far without God's help."

After their Bible study, Dr. Simons looked at his eager pupil. "Jed, I'd like to give you this map. Someday maybe you can do something about those empty spaces."

"Thank you, sir!" Jed took the special gift reverently. "Someday I hope I shall." When Jed got home, he framed the map and tacked it up carefully on the cabin wall where he could see it every day. It reminded him to ask God for guidance in his future.

3

A Hard Hunting Lesson

Every day thirteen-year-old Jed spent hours in target practice. He was growing tall and knew he was old enough to help support his family by bagging elk, deer, rabbits, and other animals that roamed the woods near Ashtabula. If he learned to shoot and bag meat it would free his father to run the trading post. Jed was determined to become a first-class hunter.

Although he studied faithfully, Jed still dreamed of someday blazing a trail across the West.

To Sally Smith's delight, a Methodist church had been organized and built in town. The Smith and Simons families became some of its most faithful worshipers.

Jed accepted Jesus Christ as his Savior and asked to join the church with his parents and brother, Ralph, and sister, Sally. He continued to learn Bible verses.

Life was full with work, worship, and study, and Jed threw himself wholly into all three.

One cold December day his father handed him the gun. "Jed, we need meat for supper. Go out to the woods and see what you can find."

Jed checked the gun carefully. As he pulled on his heavy jacket and wool cap he whistled for Wampum.

"Do you have plenty of gunpowder, Jed?" his father asked.

Jed opened the powder pouch. "All I'll need for the hunt, Pa. I'd better take my hunting knife, too."

"Be careful, son."

Jed looked at his father. "Yes, sir." He realized the dangers of the woods.

With that he set out, old Wampum sniffing ahead of him. Their footprints made purple-blue shadows on the fresh snow as they tramped toward the forest. Dark fir trees were a black smudge against the snow. Jed set his sights and checked signs. Only the faint chirp of winter birds and Wampum's soft swishy footsteps in the snow stirred the quiet winter air. Now and then small forest creatures scurried before him and vanished into the brush.

Several times Jed raised his gun to aim at a squirrel or rabbit, but each time decided to save his gunpowder for bigger game. Elk and deer were more apt to bound through small clearings.

Suddenly Jed heard a snapping sound, like a twig breaking. There, outlined against the light of a tiny clearing stood a deer. He checked his powder, took careful aim and—*Bang!* The deer jerked, crumpled to its knees, and fell on its side.

Jed skinned and dressed it. He dragged the carcass through the woods, leaving a wide trail in the snow. Mother would be pleased with fresh venison for supper.

Jed heard a sudden grunt behind him. The hair on the back of Wampum's neck stood up as he froze and growled. As Jed turned, a vicious wild hog rushed toward him, its teeth bared like fangs. Wampum threw himself on the hog. As the wild animal tore crazily at the dog, Jed dropped the deer, grabbed his gun, and cocked. Then he realized he had forgotten to reload. Holding the gun by its barrel, Jed swung it, coming down on the back of the savage beast. The boar turned from the dog, snarled at Jed, but then returned to the downed dog.

Jed remembered his hunting knife and whipped it from its sheath in his belt. With a deft slash of the sharp knife he severed the boar's hamstring. It let out a terrifying squeal, wheeled about, but fell on its disabled hindquarter. Struggling to its feet, it faced Jed, who then smacked its snout with the butt of his rifle. The boar sat back on its haunches

24

again, momentarily stunned. Finally it rose unsteadily, turned about, and hobbled away into the underbrush.

For a minute Jed stood, his chest heaving. Around him forest shadows were lengthening on the snow. Finally his brain cleared.

Old Wampum was badly hurt. Jed would have to leave the deer and carry him. He carefully picked up the old dog and began the long, slow trudge toward the cabin.

Evening shadows were beginning to merge into twilight when Jed reached home. After tending to Wampum's wounds, he told the family about his fight with the wild boar. They were amazed, for it was nothing short of a miracle that he was still alive.

"You could've been killed, Jed," his father said gently, pulling on his coat to help Jed bring home the deer.

"Yes, I know, Pa. But if I had put powder in my gun when I should have"—he looked over at the dog as it slept—"I'd have shot that beast before Wampum got hurt."

He would make sure he never forgot again.

4

Adventures on the Great Lakes

Times were hard, and Jed's father worked long hours to provide for the needs of his large family. His mother patched and repatched the children's clothes; the older boys hunted and trapped to help keep food on the table.

Fifteen-year-old Jed saw the strain on his mother's face as she struggled to take care of a family of eleven children, preparing food that always seemed in short supply, fixing clothes that always seemed like they were outgrown before they were finished. He knew he was old enough to take on more of a man's responsibility.

One day he approached his father. "Let me get a job and do my part, Father. I'm big and strong; I can help provide for my younger brothers so they can go to school instead of spending their time trapping. The boats that sail up and down the Great Lakes always hire help."

His father seemed to study the floor. Finally, he looked at Jed and said, "You're a fine son, Jedediah, and have done well in school. And you're tall for your age. I don't like to see you leave home, but as you say, we need the money. Maybe with your education you could get a job and help out."

After tearful good-byes, Jed set out on foot for Detroit—about 230 miles from home; he would use his gun to find food. Dr. Simons had written a letter of recommendation, saying that Jedediah Strong Smith was a fine young man who did well in school and was especially sharp with figures.

After a long walk Jed reached the wharf where the freight boats lay docked: He looked at the sturdy ropes (the cordelle, the French called them) used to pull the boats along the shore when the wind failed. He was strong for fifteen, but he didn't know if he was that strong. Finally he went up to the captain of a boat called the *Cheboygan* and handed him the letter from Dr. Simons.

"I sure could use a job on your boat, sir," Jed said.

"So could a lot of men, son. What can you do?"

"Well, I've hunted and trapped at home, and I know something about business. I can read and write. And I know my figures."

Captain Marks read the letter and eyed Jed shrewdly. "Hmmm. Maybe I can use you."

"Oh—and here's a sample of my hand," said Jed, taking off his hat and pulling a folded paper out of it.

"It is clear and distinct. . . . The *Cheboygan* takes supplies up and down Erie and Huron exchangin' for furs. You think you could keep record of the furs that we take in?"

"Yes, sir!"

Soon Jed was a part of the activity on the waterfront. Trappers, like French Canadians and Chippewa Indians, came with their furs when the boat reached a port. As Jock, the second mate, called out the results of the pelt count, Jed wrote it down in the logbook.

One day Jed watched Jock closely. After a while he planted his tall frame in front of Jock.

"Why don't you pay the Indians and French Canadians what you pay the British and Americans?" he demanded. "The supplies you're giving them aren't as good either."

"Don't deserve better." Jock spit. "They're just trash."

But Jed believed in fair play, so he reported this to Captain Marks. The captain was impressed with Jed's honesty and gave him even more responsibilities.

Working on the freight boats, Jed often heard the British traders talk about the fur business.

"Out West a man could get rich trapping beaver, if he doesn't get killed by Indians first."

28

Jed knew that the beaver's silky fur was much in demand back East and in Europe for making men's tall hats. Wouldn't he like to trap beaver and sell the pelts to help his family!

The men also talked about faraway rivers, like the Snake, the Yellowstone, the Musselshell, the Jefferson, the Gallatin. The names would run through Jed's mind at night as he went to sleep with the swish and splash of oars in his ears. Would he ever see those rivers?

Sometimes Jed went home between voyages. He often had long talks with Dr. Simons. The older Jed got, the more determined he became to explore the white spaces on the maps of the far West. But his family needed him, and so for the time being it was only a dream. When he wasn't on a trip with the *Cheboygan,* he trapped and sold furs.

One day in the summer of 1812, while Jed was aboard the *Cheboygan* in Lake Huron, word came that the country was at war with Great Britain and the British had already seized the *Mackinac.* This meant the *Cheboygan's* return trip to Detroit would be dangerous, since British naval ships lay waiting in the lake, just above the city.

"I know the British are running a blockade between us and Detroit," Captain Marks said, "and Indians surround the city on the land side. But somehow we must get through."

For several days the waters were quiet and they sailed without an enemy ship in sight. Lake Huron seemed deserted except for the *Cheboygan* and the gray gulls that swooped overhead. Suddenly the lookout spotted a large British naval ship behind them.

"Hoist all sails and move full speed ahead!" Captain Marks barked as the wind began to rise.

The big ship seemed to gain on them and Jed felt a shiver of fear. Would his dream of exploring the West be dashed if the *Cheboygan* sank with everyone on board?

"The ship's gaining on us, sir!" the lookout cried.

"Toward the shoreline!" the captain shouted. "Maybe they'll have second thoughts about shallows there."

By some miracle the wind dropped off to a gentle breeze

and the lake grew calm. The heavy sails of the British ship went slack; the ship slowed and then stopped.

"Let's make sure we're out of gun range!" ordered the captain.

Using all the spare hawser, the crew spliced the ropes together. They lowered a small skiff and rowed ashore. Then they pulled the *Cheboygan* hand-over-hand as they walked along the shore. Slowly the distance between the two boats widened. Jed's hands grew raw and bled as he and the other men cordelled for three hours.

Out of nowhere a wind sprang up and the men scrambled back on board, quickly hoisting the sails. A heavy black rainstorm lashed all night as the little craft sped through the darkness and downpour. They had eluded the enemy. A few nights later, under cover of darkness, the *Cheboygan* slipped past the British blockade and reached port safely.

After nearly nine years on the Great Lakes, Jed finally made up his mind to leave for the West. The trappers said trapping beaver was great along the rivers. Maybe he could make money by trapping while he explored.

On one trip home Dr. Simons reminded him, "God does not bless people who want to make money for money's sake, Jed."

"I know," Jed said quietly. "But I want to help my family. And at the same time I would like to see what lays beyond the mountains and rivers of the West."

"If it's God's will," the doctor said, "you'll be the man who explores that land."

Jed planned to complete one final trip on the *Cheboygan* before leaving for the West.

5

Down the Ohio and up the Mississippi

In the early winter of 1821 Jed finished his last trip with the *Cheboygan*. After spending some time in northern Illinois, he decided to head for Ashtabula and home. He stopped at a small bake shop and bought a bag of rolls.

Someone had dropped a newspaper on the boardwalk near the bakery door. Jed picked it up and read it while munching a sweet roll. A notice in the paper caught his eye and sent his pulse pounding—here was the answer to his prayers. It read:

To Enterprising Young Men

The subscriber wishes to engage one hundred men to ascend the river Missouri to its source, there to be employed for one, two, or three years. For particulars, enquire of Major Andrew Henry, in the County of Washington (who will ascend with and command the company) or to the subscriber near St. Louis.

WILLIAM H. ASHLEY
FEBRUARY 13, 1822

A Virginian, William Ashley had come to Missouri about the time of the Louisiana Purchase. He was a man of many vocations—a surveyor, a speculator in land, a manufacturer of gunpowder, a general merchant, militia officer, and lately lieutenant governor of Missouri. He was about to open the central region of the United States to the fur trade.

32

"That's it!" Jed cried, "It's the chance I've been waiting for."

In his buckskin pouch he carried his Bible, the yellowing ad torn from the paper, and his last pay. He hurried down the snowy trail along the shores of Lake Erie, eager to tell his parents of this chance to explore the West while trapping beaver. If he wanted to be a part of General Ashley and Major Henry's company, he had no time to lose.

After days of walking, the landmarks looked familiar. Neighbors stopped him on the way but Jed didn't talk long; he was in a hurry to get home. When he saw smoke curling from the Smith cabin he almost ran.

"Jed! Jedediah! Jed's come home!" Happy shouts greeted him.

His mother met him at the door and hugged him tightly. His father shook hands with him warmly. His brothers crowded around him, filling him in on family news: Betsy had married an Ohio boy; Eunice had married Solomon Simons; Ralph had recently married Louise Simons. The rest—Austin, Peter, Ira, Benjamin, and Nelson—eagerly plied him with questions about the fur trade on the lakes.

"What brings you home, son?" his father asked when the chatter of greetings had died down.

Jed pulled the yellowed newspaper ad from his pouch. "Here. Read this, Father."

Nelson brought his father's glasses, and Mr. Smith read the notice aloud.

"I want to answer this ad, sir," Jed said, after his father handed back the ad.

"Can't say as I blame you, son," his father said slowly. "I've always wanted to go West myself. But you just got home. Maybe if you waited until spring . . ."

Jed fidgeted nervously. "Time is running out, father. I'll have to leave tomorrow, if I want to be in the company."

"Tomorrow?" his mother asked. "Well, that doesn't give us much time, does it? I'll start packing your things right away."

That night Jed visited Dr. Simons, staying up late as they

pored over the map and talked of unknown places in the West.

The next morning Jed ate a hearty breakfast of cornbread smothered with cane molasses. He picked up the blue canvas "possibles" bag, as his mother called it because it held everything possible so you could do everything possible in every possible situation. It contained warm socks she had knitted, a new striped hickory shirt, two yellow cotton handkerchiefs, a small bottle of ink, a quill pen, a notebook in which to record his journeys, and his Bible. (Inside the Bible his mother had placed a lock of her hair, to remind him of home, she had told him.) He also had a few other books and the journal about Lewis and Clark.

While Jed checked his bag, his mother offered further suggestions of what it might include.

"I'm not going to give you a lot of advice," said his father. "You have always been a boy who could be trusted to do right. Keep your faith in God and don't forget us!"

Dr. Simons, who had come to say good-bye, held out a Methodist hymnbook.

"Sing when you're lonely, Jed," he said. "These songs will comfort you, for you will live in a wild land and meet many men who don't care about God. Don't lose your faith, whatever you do. Remember, you will make it if you always go by the grace of God."

"I'll remember," said Jed, controlling his voice. "I'll never be ashamed of God and of what I've been taught at home."

In that early March morning of 1822, Jedediah Strong Smith fastened a powder horn and pouch to his waist, slung the possibles bag on his back, and picked up his rifle. He kissed his mother and shook hands with his father. As he turned to leave, he waved good-bye to his brothers and soon disappeared among the trees as he set out on the route West.

By the time he reached Cincinnati and the Ohio River, about three hundred miles from home, it was early April. He boarded a boat just before it moved downstream toward the Mississippi and St. Louis. His blue canvas bag beside him on the forward deck, he studied the green world that

34

floated past. Splendid beeches, sycamores, and cottonwoods along the shore were starting to leaf, and here and there he saw columns of smoke feathering up from some cabin hidden in a clearing beyond the dense woods that fringed the river. Jed watched the rich bottom lands and rolling hills drift by. There was so much to see, to think about.

After the passengers ate their evening meal, a squeaking fiddle struck up a lively tune and dancers moved over the deck.

Jed, still seated beside his bag, read his Bible in the lingering twilight until darkness overtook the page. Then he rose and began to pace up and down the deck, his head bowed, his hands clasped behind him.

"What you been readin', young man?" a scrappy old man called out to him.

Jed stopped pacing. "I was reading the Great Book, sir."

"The Scriptures, eh? It's a good Book to read. Where ya headin'?"

"St. Louis."

"What you gonna do there?"

"I hope to enter the fur trade."

"I see you're somebody who knows what he wants."

Yes, Jed knew what he wanted, and in his eagerness to get there the boat seemed to be merely crawling the distance. The course of the river shifted northwest, then west, then south. Then began the most difficult part of the river trip, two hundred miles to St. Louis up the Mississippi River against the full spring flood. The cordelle was flung ashore and a dozen French boatmen began the long pull northward.

All day long the crew fought their way upstream, singing as they pulled. During the fifteen days from the mouth of the Ohio, Jed Smith learned much about up-stream travel that he would use in his adventures.

Then one day they saw the city of St. Louis rising gradually from the water's edge.

"So that's St. Louis," Jed said to a gray-bearded man on deck as the boat slowly made its way toward the wharf.

"Yessir. Has a population of five thousand folks. Got a

post office, a federal land office, two banks, a court house, a theater, three churches, a museum—and some right fine hotels!"

"You've been here before?"

"I have," the man said with a firm nod of the head. "Over there's Bloody Island."

"That sandbar?"

"Yep. Duels. . . . You gonna start a business here?"

Jed shook his head. "No, sir. I hope to join a company of trappers, General Ashley's Company, if I'm not too late."

"Well, whaddaya know!" the older man thrust out his hand. "That's exactly what I plan to do. I've been with them before. My name's John Gardner. Maybe we'll be feller-travelers to them Shining Mountains, as the Injuns call the Rockies."

"My name's Jedediah Strong Smith," Jed said, picking up his possibles bag.

"Why don't we stick together?" John said.

Jed nodded, glad he had found a friend.

After the boat docked the two men stepped ashore. The wharf was swarming with people. Businessmen in broad-cloth suits and high beaver hats were clustered in small groups talking to dark-skinned French Canadians and light-skinned Spanish. Muscular Africans and mulattoes seemed to listen to the conversations, while stolid, blanketed Indians stood apart, making no sign that they were aware of the bustle about them.

Dank, muddy smells drifted up from the river, which seemed to be drowsing in the spring sunshine. The yelling of boatmen faded and the barking of dogs rose as Jed and John Gardner started up the rutted street together.

"I know where General Ashley's office is," Gardner told Jed. "Jes' follow me."

Jed looked around, eager to see everything in the little city. The street from the levee was steep, but the two men quickly covered the distance to a fine-looking building. Gardner rapped at the door. It was opened by a huge, smiling black man.

"Hello, George!" Gardner said jovially. "I bet you didn't expect me back. Where's the General?"

The man grinned, his white teeth gleaming. "Oh, we figgered you'se comin' back, soon's you read the General's ad. Come on in."

Jed followed Gardner into General Ashley's small office. A young man about the age of Jed was seated to one side. He stood up as another older man behind a desk stood up; this man was carefully dressed in tight-fitting gray broadcloth breeches and a dark blue coat. Though he was slightly built, with a thin nose and hawk-like features, he had a distinguished bearing.

"General," Gardner said, addressing the older man, "I brought a friend to join up with you. Picked him up on the boat that brought us down the Ohio. His name's Jedediah Strong Smith. He thinks he might be one of them 'enterprisin' young men' you need."

General Ashley smiled. "Welcome. I'm glad for another recruit, although we're not having much trouble finding what we need. Young man, do you know what you're getting into?"

Jed swallowed and said quietly, "I think I do, sir."

"You look all right. I suppose you've had some experience?"

Shifting his rifle to the other arm Jed replied, "I've lived out of doors most of my life. Ever since I was fifteen I've worked as a clerk on a fur ship on the Great Lakes. I've also trapped some."

"Ever since you were fifteen, eh? How old are you now?"

"I'm almost twenty-four, sir. My father liked the frontier so we moved from New York to Pennsylvania, then to Ohio."

"Well, you don't talk like a frontiersman, Jed. You've had some education?"

Jed smiled. "I had a fine teacher, sir—Dr. Titus Simons. He got me interested in the idea of traveling into the unknown lands of the West."

"You look young, Jed. Maybe if you'd grow a beard and wear your hair longer you'd look older."

"Oh, I'm just as old whether I shave my whiskers or not."

General Ashley laughed. "I like your spirit, son. With your experience we'll be lucky to have you. We sail in two weeks. I have the feeling you're absolutely trustworthy. And with your past work as clerk, I think I'll put you in charge of buying supplies. . . . By the way, this is Thomas Fitzpatrick. He comes from a little farther east than you—Ireland—but I think you'll like him."

The young man who had risen with the general had been standing by, quiet but alert. He offered his hand and nodded. He was slender but muscular, about medium height.

After exchanging greetings, Jed, who had never had more than fifty dollars in his pocket, whistled when he saw the list of supplies General Ashley and Major Henry were asking him to buy—they totaled nearly ten thousand dollars.

Of course, bacon, coffee, calico, blankets, shirts, tobacco, and whiskey cost a great deal. Jed wished they wouldn't take whiskey, but that seemed to be one article of trade no expedition could do without. Then there were the gewgaws—cheap trade items for the Indians—ribbons, looking glasses (hand mirrors), beads, and the like.

Major Henry had left first with a group of fifty men. Jed was to be among the second group sent out by General Ashley.

One night as John Gardner and Jed walked into a cafe for supper, Jed's mind was full of the West. He would earn four hundred dollars a year, and explore the river lands besides. It was a lifelong dream come true.

The men sat down at one of the tables and Jed looked around. In the room were several long tables, as well as the bar at one end.

"What can I get you?" asked the waiter.

"Some bread and a bowl of stew."

"And would you want a bottle with that?"

Jed raised an eyebrow. "No, thank you. I don't drink whiskey, sir."

Several men lounging in the tavern began to snicker.

"It'll tighten your scalp so Injuns can't get it when you

go up the Missouri with Ashley," a man bellowed, sliding into a seat across from Jed. He held out his cup of whiskey. "Here. Drink up."

"No, thank you," Jed said, shaking his head. "I don't drink."

"Don't drink, huh?" the man said. "I think a feller who don't drink is too yaller to go up the Missouri with us. He'd turn tail and run the instant he heard a wolf howl!"

Jed's heart pounded. He tried to smile as he repeated stiffly, "No, thank you. I don't drink but I don't care if you do."

"He don't care if you drink!" another man roared. "Now ain't that somethin'?"

"Maybe I should feed you from my cup. What you got to say to that?"

Jed drew a slow deep breath. "You're more generous than wise."

"Oh, ho—you got a wit about you. But I think you're nothin' but a lily-livered coward, that's what!" said the man opposite him. "Anybody who won't drink must come from a mighty prissy family."

"You leave my family out of this!" Jed growled, anger rising in his throat. His fist shot across the table, punching the man's jaw. His head jerked back and the bench he sat on tipped over with him as he fell to the floor.

Instantly Jed was surrounded by almost a dozen mountain men, and his mouth grew dry. He started to rise slowly.

"What's going on here?" barked an authoritative voice. General Ashley had entered the tavern.

"I'm sorry, General Ashley," Jed said quietly, rising to his full height.

The crowd parted as General Ashley made his way to Jed's table.

"I shouldn't have lost my temper. But I don't like to be accused of being a coward because I don't drink and then have it blamed on my family." He paused and looked directly into the general's eyes. "Is drinking required on this job, General Ashley?"

The general looked around as he answered. "As long as you do your work, I don't care what you drink—or don't drink." Then after looking at the man sprawled on the floor, he addressed Jed, "But don't let your not drinking have the same effect as if you had been drinking . . . if you understand me, son."

"Yes, sir," said Jed, lowering his eyes. Then he nodded to General Ashley and left the tavern. John followed. Jed was quiet as they walked down the street.

When they reached a corner, John turned to Jed. "What's the matter, Jed? You're awful quiet. Still worryin' about that fight in there? It's over, so forget it."

"I'm sorry about that," Jed said again. "It's the first time I beat up anybody—and the general was right. It was as if I'd been drinking and the drink got the best of me."

"Well, you drawn your boundaries. For a man like you among men like them, it's likely that that would have to be done, sooner or later, one way or another. Besides, you weren't doin' for yourself—it was for your family."

"But I did wrong. I humiliated a man," Jed said. "God didn't put us on earth to wrong one another. It's good we ought to be doing."

John laid a hand on Jed's shoulder. "You're goin' to be in a wild country and live among rough men for the next few years. You sure you want to go up the Missouri with our kind, Jed?"

"I do," Jed said without hesitating. "I've got to go. There are lots of white spaces on the map that need to be filled. And I want to see what's really out there."

"Then so be it!"

6

Trouble on the Missouri

Dogs barked and crowds cheered as General Ashley saw
the *Enterprise* off from St. Louis that Wednesday morning
of May 8, 1822. Jed stood on deck and gazed upriver as the
keelboat was poled slowly from the dock. At last he was on
his way, headed for the country he had dreamed about for
so long. About ten miles up the Mississippi—a little less
than an average day's journey—they would meet the Missouri River and turn due west into its flow.

The seventy-five-foot long *Enterprise* was heavily loaded
with ten thousand dollars worth of supplies for the trappers:
food, traps, knives, fishhooks, files, rifles, bullets, powder,
and repair parts. In addition, gewgaws were carried for
trade with the Indians.

The keelboat was only some twenty feet wide. It was a
ribbed craft built on a keel covered with planks. The draft
was very shallow, and most of the deck was covered by a
long box-like structure, which held the cargo. Along each
side of this structure, from bow to stern, there was a narrow
path, about two or three feet wide.

When the wind was right—which was seldom—a tall
square sail was hoisted from a masthead that stood about
a third of the way from the bow. In the deep water, a dozen
oars between the cargo box and the stern might be used,
but in shallow water, oars were used with difficulty, if at
all. When the current grew swift and strong against the
boat, the crew had to resort to the cordelle. Along the bank,

41

inch by inch, foot by foot, crashing through underbrush below rocky bluffs, slogging through marsh that sloped away from the river, they dragged the boat upstream.

Among the hundred or so "enterprising young men" were twenty French boatmen whose job it was to take the boat to its destination. They walked along the deck, pushing the boat along by means of poles thrust against the river's bottom. If the wind was right, the boatmen would hoist the big square sail to take the boat up the river. Jed grew wide-eyed at the scenery that spilled out ahead of him. He watched great white birds glide slowly ahead of the keelboat. Catbirds scolded among the willows, and now and then strange, gorgeous green birds soared overhead.

He noticed that the shores along the Missouri River were not like the serene forests of the East. The low banks of the river were covered with tall timber, sometimes interlaced with wild grapevines and tangled brush. Often enormous fallen trees were piled on one another and were overgrown with nettles. Wood ticks burrowed into his skin and heavy swarms of mosquitoes left welts that burned for days.

Occasionally an Indian dugout passed them on the river. These graceful boats were used by the Iowas, Sacs, and Kaws in the area.

As Jed stood at the bow of the boat, facing upstream, the wind blew through his brown hair. His blue eyes strained for a glimpse of the Shining Mountains of the Rockies. Someday he would go beyond them and come back to tell what he had seen.

I'll keep careful records, he promised himself, *and make accurate maps. Maybe I can even write a book about my findings—like Lewis and Clark.*

Since Jed had been both clerk and hunter for the *Cheboygan,* General Ashley had told Daniel Moore, the captian of the *Enterprise,* to excuse him from the heavy work of helping on the boat. He was to help supply fresh meat, keep a record of the trip, and reckon wages.

All day long the crew battled the wind and swift current and avoided hidden rocks and submerged trees, or "sawyers," as they were called. Sometimes the river grew treacherous. The boatmen stumbled along the slippery banks, climbed over rocks, and plowed through willows. Often they waded hip deep through the muddy water. Yet they sang hour after hour as they pulled the boat along.

The *Enterprise* was now nearing the Missouri-Nebraska border. The churning yellow-gray water had made it difficult to spot shoals, and they had had to skirt deadly snags and sawyers. But they had succeeded in traveling over three hundred miles from St. Louis.

One of the men on the trip was Jim Clyman, six years older than Jed. He had been a mounted ranger during the War of 1812. He was tall and thin, with sharp features. His black eyes were alert under his bushy eyebrows.

One day Jim took Jed and Big Art Black, a man of unusual size and strength, ashore for some hunting. "Enough of hardtack, beans, and salt pork," said Jim.

Soon they had shot an elk and a deer, and the next day they killed a black bear and several wild turkeys.

Jim, Jed, and Art were just getting back to the river from a hunting trip one day. They looked up just as the *Enterprise* swung slowly around a bend in the river. Suddenly the boat veered and the mast was thrown against an overhanging limb of a tree. The boat spun sideways in the swift current and, as water rushed across its deck, flipped over.

"It's gonna sink for sure!" Art shouted.

The boatmen on shore dropped the cordelle and dove into the water to save what they could. The men on the boat fought for shore.

Jed, Art, and Jim raced toward the river. They dropped their guns and game, pulled off their buckskin shirts, and jumped into the stream to help save supplies.

"Look, Jed!" Moses "Black" Harris yelled. "There goes your plunder bag, Book, writin's and all!"

Jed plunged into the swirling water. Ahead, he saw his blue possibles bag bobbing up and down. It wasn't easy to swim in the rushing river; he had to fight hard to reach the bag. Suddenly he got caught on a snag. Just when he thought he would go under, he jerked himself free. A foot or two ahead was his bag, caught in the branch of a half-buried tree. He reached out and grabbed it and then felt himself go under.

Art grabbed him and pulled him ashore. When Jed opened his eyes he saw the anxious face of his friend John Gardner and the worried brown eyes of Moses Harris. He sat up and looked at them with a lopsided grin.

"Are you all right?" Captain Moore called out from a promontory on the bank at the spot the boat had gone down.

"Yes, sir," Jed said. "I'm fine."

"And so's his Book," shouted Moses Harris. Then to Jed he said, with a big toothy grin, "I thought you was already baptised, boy."

The men walked slowly to the place where the *Enterprise* was now sinking out of sight. Trappers and boatmen sorted through the pitiful pile of cargo they had been able to salvage from the treacherous river.

All the men were safe, but most of the supplies and trading goods had sunk to the bottom of the Missouri. A few articles still tossed about in the powerful current.

Jed stared at the spot the boat went down.

John Gardner ambled up behind him and laid a hand on his shoulder. "You okay, son? You look kinda sick."

"How did it happen, John?" he asked.

Gardner shook his gray head. "That boat just rounded the bend. Cap'n Moore was a-watchin' the current that was rollin' up alongside and he couldn't look both ways at once. The mast caught on a low-hangin' limb and flipped the *Enterprise* right over. Next thing we knowed, we was swimmin' for our lives."

"And ten thousand dollars lost!" Jed added in awe. "Do you think General Ashley will call off the expedition?"

Before Gardner could answer, Captain Moore came up beside them. "I've got to get word to General Ashley right away. That man'll want to send a new boat and supplies to get the trappers to the mountains in order to get enough beaver before winter sets in. But I doubt that I'll come back. I've had enough of this cantankerous river!"

He said whoever wanted to return with him to St. Louis was welcome. "Jim, if you're bent on stayin', I'll put you in charge here."

Around the campfire that night there was much talk about getting back to civilization. Some men suggested that the trip wasn't worth it. But in the end, only three chose to return to St. Louis with Captain Moore.

Jed sat alone reading his Bible, as was his custom. He was looking to the Lord for guidance after the day's great loss. He hoped General Ashley wouldn't quit the trip.

But when Jim talked about life on the upper Missouri, Jed laid down his Bible and listened. Jim stroked his beard as he talked about Indians and how they would protect themselves in case of an attack. Some of the men admitted they needed target practice to improve their aim.

"I see how we'll spend our time until General Ashley sends more supplies," Jim said. "We have enough powder left. Tomorrow we begin target practice."

Three weeks later General Ashley himself came upstream in a new keelboat with forty-five new recruits. *He isn't going to quit!* thought Jed. And to top it off, they brought plenty of Irish potatoes and coffee to add to their monotonous diet of meat and berries.

That night the men licked their fingers over a feast of meat and potatoes, washed down with scalding coffee. The next morning the expedition was ready to leave, on its way West once more.

7

"Watch out for the Rees!"

After breakfast, the struggle against the Missouri began again. As the new keelboat pushed up the river, the work grew harder. The back-breaking toil at the cordelle, the oars, and the poles was wearing out the boatmen; they began to grumble instead of sing. It had been slow, difficult work before; now it became even harder.

Trappers who met Ashley's party along the way filled their minds with stories of savage Indians and fierce grizzly bears. Men began to drop out and start back for St. Louis.

One night a heavy canoe arrowed downstream and pulled ashore alongside the keelboat. Four bearded trappers climbed out for a drink of coffee.

"I'm Joe Beecher," said the tall one. "We've been playin' hide-and-seek with the Blackfeet for a year now and we're lookin' to settle down in St. Louis for a spell."

General Ashley introduced himself, adding, "Well, the Blackfeet don't make a man feel welcome . . . and maybe with good cause. But I'm sorry to hear you're heading downriver. I sure could use at least four good men."

The Rocky Mountain fur trade was carried on by powerful, well-organized companies or partnerships (like Ashley's) as well as by free trappers, men who worked on their own, furnished their own equipment, trapped where they pleased, and sold their furs to whoever paid them the most. On occasion free trappers would sign up with a company for a time.

"We're meeting my partner, Major Andrew Henry, on the Yellowstone," said General Ashley.

"He's an outstandin' mountain man," Jim Clyman put in.

"And who might you be?" asked Beecher.

"Sorry, gentlemen. I forgot my manners. This is Jim Clyman, my recruiter."

The four men looked at each other. Finally one of them asked, "What're you payin'?"

"Four hundred a year," said General Ashley.

That night four more men were added to the Ashley expedition.

A day later they reached the Platte River. Above the Platte lay Fort Atkinson at Old Council Bluffs, the farthest army post on the Missouri. Here Lewis and Clark had held a council with the chiefs of several Indian tribes. *Wouldn't Dr. Simons like to see this site!* thought Jed.

Now the heavily wooded forests gave way to prairie country with billowing grass, waist high. One day a sudden rainstorm blew down from dark skies. The crew worked hard to bring the boat ashore in the howling wind that pushed a wall of water on them. For hours one crash of thunder followed another.

The next day the battered crew pushed on to the mouth of the Big Sioux River, where the American Fur Company had a trading post. Although there was rivalry between the fur companies that trapped along the rivers, they respected each other. Here the men rested for several hours, then the boat struggled upriver once more into Sioux Indian country.

When a dozen Sioux Indians appeared suddenly on the banks of the Missouri, Jim Clyman and General Ashley went ashore to smoke the peace pipe with them. Jed watched the Indians from the deck. They were at least six feet tall. Several wore eagle feather bonnets and grizzly-bear claws around their necks.

"What if Jim and the General are in danger?" asked one of the men.

"How long you been on the river, man? Even we've heard about Jim Clyman, how he knows the way to talk with the

48

Indians!" exclaimed Joe Beecher. "The Sioux are powerful fighters, but they've been friendly with trappers. They're not likely to cause trouble unless they have a reason—not like the Blackfeet. They're the orneriest Indians alive."

When Jim and General Ashley returned several hours later, Jim said, "We traded some tobacco and mirrors with the chiefs for some advice."

"What kind of advice?" Joe Beecher asked.

"They said to watch out for the Rees. They've gone into Sioux country and have attacked small parties of trappers."

"We'll see about that," Joe said. "We reach the Ree villages in a few days."

In early September Ashley's party reached the villages of the Arickarees, or Rees, as they were nicknamed. The villages were on the left side of the river, about a quarter of a mile apart. The huts were round and made of poles, split timber, mud, and grass.

General Ashley took Jim Clyman, Joe Beecher, and Jed Smith ashore with him for a council with the Ree chiefs.

Jed studied their faces, which were colored with green stain and charcoal. On their shoulders they wore buffalo skins, the hairy side turned in and the skin side sketched with paintings of animals and men. A folded red cloth was tucked around their legs and they wore moccasins of deer and elkskin. Jed noticed that their leggings had tufts of human hair.

As Jed sat down with the others on a buffalo skin in the council lodge, Chief Gray Eyes lighted the peace pipe with a coal from the fire, pointed it toward the sky, to each of the four corners of the earth, and to the ground. Then he passed the pipe to the subchief on the left. Each chief took a puff.

Jim Clyman was the only one who understood the Ree language, and he translated their words into English.

"Tell him," General Ashley said, "that our hearts are good. That we want peace and will trade goods for horses."

Jim talked to Gray Eyes, then turned to the General. "Gray Eyes says, 'Our hearts are good too, and we too want peace.' He has agreed to trade for horses. But first he wants us to eat with him."

Jed's stomach churned when Jim grinned and whispered that they were being served roast dog. But he knew he couldn't insult the chief by refusing his food. Pemmican helped take away the dog taste. And the dried corn was tasty. In later years Jed would look upon dog as something of a delicacy.

After the feast, the trading began. Soon General Ashley had the fifty horses he wanted. He brought out the trade goods—brightly-colored cloth, knives, bridles, spurs, tomahawks, kettles—and gave all the chiefs presents of gewgaws: looking glasses, tobacco, chocolate, beads, face paint, whistles, seashells.

As his men bunched the horses on shore that night, Jim warned Ashley to double the number of horse guards. "Gray Eyes talked a lot about bein' friendly," he said, "but he may send some warriors to take back a few horses if we don't watch out."

The group had already traveled more than fifteen hundred miles by water. Now that they had horses, General Ashley decided to split his party. He took some of the men overland, by horseback, toward the mouth of the Yellowstone. Jed was with this group. On Tuesday, October 1, 1822, the party reached its destination and built a rough stockade, calling it Fort Henry. At its completion the men shouted, fired their guns, and threw their hats in the air. As Jed's came floating down he caught it on his gun barrel, bowing to Art Black who had clapped in mock admiration at the feat. At last Jed was in the country he had dreamed about as a child.

While the men told tall tales and sang hilarious songs around the campfire, Jed read his Bible, every once in a while finding in his hand the brown strand of hair his mother had placed in his Bible. Finally he picked up the book about the Lewis and Clark expedition that Dr. Simons had given him. The Rockies, the Indians' "Shining Mountains," couldn't be too much farther.

8

Learning to Trap

As autumn blazed among the tamarisk and wild plums along the river, General Ashley and Major Henry made plans for fall trappings. They looked forward to a good season on beaver streams near the Missouri and Yellowstone rivers. Fortunately, the savage Blackfeet had remained quiet for several months. Henry's men had already gathered a number of packs of furs to be shipped with General Ashley when he returned to St. Louis before winter.

"Jim Clyman and Jed Smith," Ashley said, "I need you to go down the Yellowstone and shoot a good supply of meat for the fort. After that, you can join the rest of the trappers on the beaver trail."

As the two men walked along the river, Jed saw the yellow cliffs that gave the river its name. Sure-footed Rocky Mountain sheep with huge horns leaped along the rim of the cliffs, and many deer, rabbits, and squirrels bounded through the thickets.

"We'll find plenty of meat," Jim said.

During Jed and Jim's hunt, Major Henry sent one party to the Powder River country and another up the Missouri as far as Milk River.

When the two hunters returned to the fort with the supply of game, they started up the Missouri to join their trapping party. Winter was coming, and a sharp wind howled out of the north. Jed was thankful for his warm clothes.

He wore fringed buckskin clothes from his neck to his

knees. Jim had told him to cover his knees to his ankles with bright red wool cloth. On his head perched a jaunty fur cap (later he would find a bandanna more comfortable in hot weather) and on his feet he wore moccasins made of a single piece of buckskin. He carried a butcher knife, hatchet, two pistols, and his possibles bag. In it he had flint and steel to build a fire, an awl for punching holes in leather, and buckskin to repair his moccasins. There were fishhooks, needles, and other odds and ends. He made sure he never went without his powder horn and bullet pouch. And of course, he always carried his Bible, hymnbook, journals, and other materials.

The two moved carefully along the small rushing creeks that flowed into the Missouri, looking for beaver signs. Jim showed Jed a dam that beavers had built to make a pond. On the edge of the pond they had also built a lodge of small branches and mud.

The water was icy, and as Jed waded upstream his feet grew numb and he shivered. "That's the bad part about trapping," Jim told him. "You gotta wade in cold water. Sure, it makes your joints kinda stiff, but you have to go in the water, or the beaver will smell you and get away."

Jim took a five-pound steel trap, which trailed a five-foot chain, spread its jaws wide, and set the trap's trigger. Then he baited the trap by dipping a twig in oil from the castor gland of a beaver and fixing it so that it was just a few inches above the water where the trap lay just a few inches below the water. After cutting a stout pole, he picked up the chain and walked toward the middle of the stream. Then he drove the pole through a ring on the end of the chain and into the bed of the creek.

"When the beaver tries to get that perfumed twig, he'll step in the trap and then try to make for the bank. This pole'll keep him from gettin' the trap up the bank. If the beaver gets on the bank he'll gnaw his foot off and get away, and you gotta drown a beaver quick if you catch him."

When the trap was set, Jim splashed water on the bank

52

to wash away any human scent. Then he and Jed plodded upstream to set another trap.

Jed's first beaver was about three feet long and weighed about thirty-five pounds. "About average," said Jim. Its scaly, paddle-like tail was four inches wide and eighteen inches long. It was this tail, Jed learned, that made the beaver a good swimmer. To his amazement, the tail was very tasty, once the scaly skin was burned off and the meat was boiled.

By now Jed and Jim had caught up with the rest of the trappers. Each evening they set their traps, and every morning they had usually caught several beavers. The trappers skinned the animals, scraping the flesh and fat from the pelts before stretching them on willow frames to dry. After the pelts were dry, they were pressed into packs, each weighing about a hundred pounds.

"Now I see why trappers need horses!" Jed told Jim after their pile of skins grew heavy.

As Jim and Jed worked the stream together, Jim taught him many things. "Remember, Jed, we're in Blackfeet country. If you don't keep your eyes and ears open, you won't live long," Jim warned. "When you move upstream, watch the water for a sign of somethin' ahead of you."

"And if you follow a trail," Jed added, "watch for a blade of grass that's pressed down or a leaf that's turned. I learned something about tracking Indians back in Ohio. Like trail signs, tree blazes, stone signs, grass signs. Stuff like that."

"Right," Jim said. "Remember that if you spot wild animals that are runnin' or birds actin' excited, be on the lookout for Blackfeet."

As the two men walked down the trail, Jim told him more. "When you're travelin' with a horse or mule, watch 'em close. There's a scent about the grease the Indians wear that cantankers an animal, and it'll let you know when an Indian's around."

Jim taught him other things, too. "The old Indian sign for peace is to clasp your hands in front of your body, usually left and down. A written sign is three angles all pointin' one way, like this." Jim squatted on the ground and drew the sign in the dirt. "The war sign goes this way, like angles goin' in different directions. A broken pipe means 'peace not kept.'

"And they use other signs to mean somethin'. When they pat their stomachs it means the meal was good. The sign for *pay* is you hold out your hand half open and rub your forefinger and thumb together."

"Say, that's interesting," Jed said. "I guess I'd better learn all I can, since I'll probably run across Indians in my exploring."

"That you will, Jed," Jim said with a grin. "That you will."

For the next hour Jim showed him other ways Indians communicate with each other, and with white men. He also taught Jed a little Chinook jargon, a simplified language based on Chinook and using English, French, and other Indian words. Jed tried to remember all he could.

No wonder Jim Clyman had survived the war as a mounted ranger. His sharp eye had come to read every bush, rock, and tree; he could lie motionless as a stick and study the trail for hours. Even when he slept, one ear seemed cocked for any sound. When he awoke, he was instantly alert. Jed admired this rugged friend.

I've got to be alert like Jim, Jed told himself. *If I want to trap in Indian country, I've got to learn all the ways of the Indians and the tricks of the trapping trade.*

Sometimes Jed burst into a hymn as he and Jim rode along. "A good doctor once prescribed it—it keeps me from getting lonely," he told Jim.

The trappers didn't stay long in any one spot but moved on as soon as they had trapped in one creek for a few days. When they reached the mouth of the Musselshell River, it was time to build shanties and settle in for the cold season.

Before long, the winter winds blew in bitterly cold and the Missouri River froze solid. But the men were snug and warm in their shanty camp.

When the snow fell and winds howled along the river, the trappers slept a good deal, for there was little to do. Some-

54

times they told stories around the campfire. Jed read his Bible, wrote in his journals, and thought of his family far away in Ohio. His rowdy friends had already learned that this quiet Christian had plenty of courage and that he never lost his head in danger.

One day hundreds of buffalo thundered across the ice. The men shot as many as they could, and every night humps boiled and ribs sputtered and roasted over the open fire.

Jim taught Jed about the uses of the buffalo. "He's a mighty useful critter. The hair on his head is thick and springy and it makes a good pillow. The fur's as soft as lamb's wool and it makes a robe that's light but real warm."

Jed watched as Jim cut strips of buffalo meat an inch thick and then spread the strips on poles to dry.

"What are you doing, Jim?" Jed asked.

"Makin' jerky. . . . The wind and sun will dry this batch in about five days. I'll build a smoky fire under another batch and it'll dry in three. Wood smoke makes mighty sweet-tastin' jerky."

"What about pemmican," Jed asked, "like we had with the Rees? Now that was real tasty!"

"Well," Jim said, "you need jerky to make pemmican." He took a piece of jerky and scraped away all the tough parts, then pounded the meat with a stone until it was powdery, almost like flour. Next he tamped the powder loosely in a large rawhide bag and poured melted fat over it. Then he handed it to Jed.

"Here's your pemmican, Jed. It'll keep sweet in this bag for a long time. Pemmican is the best food there is when you're goin' strong. It sticks to your ribs and gives you strength. . . . Of course, berry pemmican's best of all. Indian squaws make it by poundin' dried wild cherries or some other fruit into the jerky. But that is a lot of bother on the trail."

Spring broke slowly, with faint bursts of green, and finally the huge cakes of ice crackled and crashed against each other like booming cannons.

The men grew impatient to move on. Snow still lay in

55

patches on the ground when Jim and Jed led the trapping party back down the Missouri to the mouth of the Yellowstone. A handful of trappers were at Fort Henry when the party arrived. General Ashley was still gone, they were told, but he would return from St. Louis before long with another party of trappers, and Major Henry was off along the Powder River trapping beaver.

Jim Clyman frowned. "I'm afraid Major Henry's goin' to be in trouble," he said. "The Blackfeet have been too quiet and that's not like them. He's right in the middle of Blackfeet country."

A few days later Major Henry and a dozen exhausted trappers dragged into the fort. The Major's arm was in a sling. Others straggled in several days later. Some were wounded and ten were missing. Only a few pack horses had been rescued from the marauding Blackfeet.

"The Blackfeet attacked our camp near Great Falls," the Major said. "My men saved themselves only by riding away fast. I killed one Blackfoot but got hurt. I'm not retreating farther. We'll wait here for General Ashley. He was to have left St. Louis in early March with two keelboats."

"Maybe someone should go downriver and hurry him along," Jim suggested.

"Good idea," Major Henry said. "Why don't you go, Jim? You know the country." Jim glanced at Jed. "I will, if I can take Jed Smith with me. He's turnin' into a real good mountain man."

"So you haven't had your fill of adventure, eh, Jed?"

Jim smiled and shook his head.

A day or so later Jim and Jed mounted two good horses and were on their way.

Jim planned to hit the Missouri River somewhere near the mouth of the Cheyenne. And Jim's judgment was so good that what he guessed was usually better than most men knew.

"Look!" yelled Jed. "There they are!" Two keelboats moved slowly up the quiet gray-brown river.

9

A Battle with the Rees

"I didn't expect to see you men so soon," said General Ashley. "What brings you down this way?"

Jim's dark eyes narrowed and he jerked his head in the direction they had come from. "The Blackfeet are in a foul mood, General. Major Henry ran into a surly tribe and lost ten men. He thought it would be a good idea if you knew how things were."

"Well, you're not the only ones with bad news," Ashley said. "We've met trappers who say that the Rees are also in a mean mood. One band of Rees moved into Sioux country and killed a party of fur traders. Then they attacked Fort Recovery and the son of the Ree chief was killed. Now they're out for revenge. To top it off, the Rees plan to join the Mandans to fight any trappers on their way to the Yellowstone."

Jim whistled. "We are in an awful fix. We can't go overland to the Yellowstone unless we have pack horses. And the Rees are the only Indians around here who can let us have them."

"What do you suggest, Jim?" General Ashley asked, a worried frown tracking across his forehead.

Jim took a long deep breath. "We'll just have to keep goin' and take a chance on their stayin' friendly."

"I agree," the general replied. "We'll just have to talk peace with the Rees."

On Friday, May 30, 1823, the keelboats rounded the bend

in the river near the Ree villages. The ninety men aboard were an unruly lot, not given to obeying orders, maybe not dependable in a fight. Still, the horses were desperately needed if the party was to slip past the treacherous Blackfeet upriver.

Jim Clyman shook his head as he pointed to the high ground above the river. "Take a look, Jed. The Rees have built a palisade of logs around their villages! That could mean they're spoilin' for a fight."

Slowly the boats moved nearer the shore, then stopped. General Ashley took Jim, Jed, and several others in a small skiff and rowed ashore to talk to the Indians.

"The white men come in peace," Jim told them in the Chinook language. "They want to trade for horses."

Three Indians came out of their lodges and stood with arms folded, then silently squatted on the sandy beach. General Ashley, Jim, and Jed sat down with them.

After the peace pipe was passed, Jim began to speak for General Ashley.

"White chief's heart is good and he speaks with a straight tongue," Jim said slowly, carefully. "White chief sorry that son of Ree chief was killed in trouble at Fort Recovery. White chief hopes that Rees will not hold it against all white men."

He paused and looked toward General Ashley. "White chief is great man and the men on boat shoot straight. If there is trouble, many Rees could die. That would not be right, because white chief wants peace. He wants to trade for horses again to take to friends on the Yellowstone."

The Rees listened silently, their black eyes stony. Then they walked apart for council and talked together for a long time.

Jed felt sweat trickling down the small of his back. He glanced at Jim. The mountain man's eyes were closed. He wondered if he was praying. It was time for it. General Ashley sat fingering his belt, saying nothing.

Finally the chiefs returned. They were sorry, they said, about what had happened down river. But that was long

58

ago and they were ready to forget. They were willing to trade their good horses to the white men.

General Ashley nodded. "Good!" It seemed all their worries were over, and they brought out the gewgaws.

But Jim muttered, "Better keep your eyes open. The Rees can't be trusted."

For the next day or two on the beach trading went on. The Rees and the trappers haggled over each scrappy Indian pony. The Rees drove a hard bargain: They would take only powder and bullets for the animals.

"I don't like that at all," Jim said, shaking his head. "We could get those bullets right back!"

On June 1, General Ashley had traded for enough horses. He ordered Jim, Jed, and forty reliable men to start the animals across country to the Yellowstone River in the morning. Meanwhile, they were to remain with the horses on the beach overnight. The men hobbled the animals so they couldn't wander away.

A few white men joined the feast at the Ree villages that night. Drums boomed and there was much noisy singing and dancing. It bothered Jim, so he rowed to the keelboat to speak to General Ashley.

"I don't like the sound of those drums, General," he said. "There's something nasty afoot."

"Well, I'm not expecting a fight," Ashley said cheerfully. "They seemed peaceable enough when we traded."

"But I think it's a mistake to camp on the beach, sir," Jim continued. "If the Rees start a fight, we'll be pushed into the river and lose the horses."

"Don't worry. I don't think that will happen."

When Jim returned to the beach he motioned to Jed. "Ashley's not figuring on trouble, but I am. Go tell the men to stay awake tonight and keep their guns loaded and handy. We may not be able to save our horses but we'll sure make it rough for the Rees, if we have to."

Finally the drums quieted and the village grew silent. After midnight heavy black clouds rolled across the sky and lightning forked as thunder grumbled. Soon rain fell in sheets from the sky. The horses became excited and Jim sent more guards to calm them.

About three o'clock a horse guard rushed up to Jim. "One of the men . . . just came back . . . from the Ree villages," he panted. "He thinks the Indians are getting ready to attack. They've already killed one of our men . . ."

Jim's face darkened with anger. "Hurry and tell General Ashley to get ready for trouble," he barked.

Jed quickly checked the men on the beach. By now the rain had slowed to a mist but the night was still and black as a gopher hole. Crouching behind a log, he peered into the darkness. The silence from the village was ominous. After a while the rain stopped and a pale pink dawn crept into the sky. The horse herd was quiet now, but Jed's finger tightened on his rifle. He hoped there would be no fight.

General Ashley rowed ashore and marched boldly uphill toward the Ree village to demand the body of the dead man and ask for custody of his murderer.

Jim Clyman was aghast. "Is the man crazy!" he shouted as he rushed after General Ashley and jerked him back toward the boat.

He was answered by a puff of smoke from the Ree palisades, followed by the crack of rifles.

"Get behind the horses," Jed called to the horse guards. "They're attacking!"

The whole palisade seemed to spout smoke and fire at once. Horses lunged around in their hobbles, screaming as they dropped to the sand.

As the attack intensified, Jed turned his attention to the horses. More animals were dropping each minute; dodging among them, he unhobbled as many as he could. If this continued, the Rees would wipe out the entire herd. He tried to drive them into the river but as the Ree rifles kept on firing, horse after horse fell screaming and kicking on the sand.

It was hopeless. Jed saw that the horses couldn't be saved, so he hurried back to help the men fight.

"Into the river, quick!" Jed shouted. "Swim to the keelboats. We can't fight them behind their stockade."

General Ashley, back at the keelboat, ordered the French boatmen to help the trappers, but they refused. They were willing to work on the cordelle, they said, but fighting Indians wasn't their job.

Finally a few men in a canoe splashed ashore to help the men pinned down by the Rees' fire. As many as possible were pulled into the canoe.

One man described it later:

"When his party was in danger, Mr. Smith was always foremost to meet it, and the last man to flee. Those who saw him at the Rickaree fight in 1823 can attest to the truth of this assertion."

As soon as all the swimmers were on the keelboats, Ashley ordered the captain to fall back downstream. On board, the beaten men examined their wounds and counted their losses. Two had drowned while swimming, and others had been shot while trying to retreat. In all, twelve men had been lost and eleven wounded. Two died later. Only a few horses made it across to the opposite shore.

John Gardner, who had been Jed's first friend before beginning the expedition, was most seriously wounded. Jed thought of the time they had met on the way to St. Louis and of John's kindness to him. Now his old friend was dying.

John Gardner motioned to Jed and Hugh Glass, "I'm . . . not going to make it," he gasped. "My folks are old now. They'd like me to have a Christian burial. Will you . . . pray over my grave, Jed?"

Jed nodded and opened his Bible. "Remember, John, the Great Book says, 'For God so loved the world, that he gave his only begotten Son, that whosoever believeth in him should not perish but have everlasting life.' Believe and accept it, my friend."

John Gardner nodded faintly. "I . . . believe, Jed. Tell my folks—" He gasped again and lay still.

At John Gardner's burial on a small island, Jedediah Smith read several verses of assurance and comfort from the Bible. Then he prayed a moving, powerful prayer "to the God in whose sternness all were prepared to believe, and in whose compassion at this moment they much needed to believe." It was a sobering time for the remaining band clustered around the dead trapper as they bowed their heads and listened to Jed's prayer.

Hugh Glass wrote to John Gardner's family:

> My painful duty it is to tell you of the death of your son which befell at the hands of the Indians on the second day of June in the early morning. He lived a little while after he was shot and asked to inform you of his sad fate. We brought him to the ship where he soon died. Mr. Smith, a young man of our company, made a powerful prayer that moved us greatly, and I am persuaded John died in peace. His body is buried with the others near this camp and his grave marked with a log. His things will be sent to you . . .

A gloom settled over the small group of survivors that huddled on the keelboats after the funeral. What did their future hold now? Escape past the Ree villages along the Missouri was almost impossible. Would they be forced to go back to St. Louis? Was Jed's dream of going beyond the Shining Mountains to be wiped out in one stroke by a savage Indian war?

10

"I'll Go"

General Ashley's plight was desperate. He had to pass the Ree towns or turn his keelboats back to St. Louis. More than a dozen of his men were dead and some men were wounded. Furthermore, forty-three men wished to desert.

"I agree, we can't go past the Ree villages at this point," he told his few faithful followers. "So we'll try to move back down the Missouri to the mouth of the Cheyenne. Now I need someone to take a message to Major Henry and ask him to join us. Then we'll plan our next move. But it will be a dangerous overland trip to Fort Henry. Who'll volunteer to go?"

Jed stepped forward quickly. "I'll go."

"So will I," Jim said behind him.

"Thank you, Jed and Jim," General Ashley said. "But I can't spare two of my best men. But since you're younger and have been over the territory, Jed, I'll let you go. You'll find your own way, but you can't go alone. There may be other Indians out that way."

"Gen'l Ashley," a soft voice spoke up. "I weel go weeth him."

The volunteer was Pierre, a French-Canadian trapper who had joined Ashley at Fort Recovery. "I can smell Indian two-three mile away."

"Good," said Ashley. "I appreciate that." Then he smiled slightly and said, "How soon can you start?"

Just as quickly, Jed answered, "Tonight . . . after we round up some horses and pack our grub."

At dark, Jed and Pierre mounted their shaggy ponies and left quietly. Traveling light, each man carried a rifle, a pistol, a butcher knife, corn dodgers, and jerky. As always, Jed's possibles bag was strapped on his back. With only the soft rustle of coarse grass underfoot, they rode all night, slipping quietly past the Ree villages without being spotted.

When they reached the Grand River in the morning, Pierre pointed to a strip of timber on the right. "You theenk we stop awhile?" he asked.

"Yes," Jed said. "We can both use a bit of rest and a bite to eat."

The two men tied their horses and stretched out on the soft grass.

"Indians smell smoke two-three mile away," Pierre said. They ate a cold breakfast.

"We'll rest for an hour," Jed said after breakfast. "But let's keep our horses saddled."

To Jed it seemed they had slept only a few minutes when one of the horses whinnied. He sprang to has feet and grabbed his rifle, and Pierre scrambled up immediately. The sun was dipping westward—they had slept much longer than the hour they had planned.

Horses can smell an Indian, Jim Clyman had said. Was this why the pony had neighed?

Pierre and Jed crouched low, slipped to the edge of the grove, and looked around. To the east they saw a band of twenty-five Indians riding down a steep bluff into the valley, not more than half a mile away. The Indians then spread out, heading toward the birches where Jed and Pierre had camped.

"They know we're here," Jed whispered, "but they're taking their time because they don't know how many of us there are. Let's get away before they find out."

Seconds later, Jed and Pierre were galloping away. After a mile, they urged their mounts into the river. Behind them they heard shouts of Indians splashing in after them.

All evening Jed and Pierre rode hard. Only when it grew dark and the stars began to wink did they stop to rest their horses.

Pierre dropped to the ground and listened. "I theenk Indians three-four mile away," he said with a quiet nod.

"Well, we'd better move on," Jed said, "because they don't know we're ahead. We'll lead the horses to give them a bit more rest."

A few minutes later Pierre sniffed. "Smoke . . . up ahead. Maybe Rees."

"Stay here with the horses," Jed said, picking up his rifle. He moved softly down the valley and crept cautiously around the bluff on the right. About a hundred yards ahead he noticed the dull glow of a camp fire in a small thicket. As he crawled toward the fire, he would feel the path ahead of him for any dry twigs. As he peered through a clump of bushes he saw a Ree near the fire.

The Indian was resting his chin on his chest, ready to fall asleep. Another Ree was stretched out on the ground beside him. Jed heard the snort of horses among the trees. He shook his head slowly, closing his eyes for a moment. *We can't risk trying to slip past them, not with others right behind us.*

Every second counted. Carefully he checked his rifle and pistol. He lay down on the ground, putting his pistol beside him. Aiming at the Ree sitting near the fire, he shot. Then he picked up his pistol and sprang forward. The first Ree had fallen onto his comrade, now struggling to reach his rifle. But Jed shot him before he knew what had happened.

By the time Pierre rushed through the brush, Jed had caught the Indian ponies. "What you do?" Pierre asked. "Ree shoot at you?"

"No, I shot at them," he said dryly. "Take a horse."

"You be all right?"

"No."

"Ah, because you kill Indian?"

"Two—two Indians."

65

"You theenk God have Indian in mind when he say not to kill?"

"Your Franciscans and Jesuits seem to think so."

"Me? I don't know. I do know they kill me, I kill them." Pierre, taking the reins of the horse in one hand, pulled out his knife with the other."

"No!" Jed thundered. "It's bad enough to kill. Taking their scalps makes us worse than them; we're the civilized ones."

Pierre stared at him. "But mountain men, they all take scalps like Indians."

"No," Jed said quietly. "Not all."

Shaking his head, Pierre mounted the horse.

Six hours later the men found a blueberry thicket and made camp. After staking out their ponies to graze, they slept by turns.

As darkness began to filter through the twilight, the two men started out again. Near midnight they reached the fork of the Grand River.

"This river's as crooked as a dog's hind leg," Jed said. "We'll leave it and head out across the prairie. We can follow the North Star."

Jogging across the prairies they were soon in trouble, for the sky darkened and a late spring rain began to fall. They could no longer see the North Star as they slogged through the downpour. Pulling their blankets over their heads while chewing on corn dodgers and jerky, they rode across the soggy land, wondering if they were going in circles.

The prairie had become a swamp and the horses' hooves sank in deeply. Several times Jed and Pierre dismounted to let the animals rest, leading them through the muck. Now the mud sucked at their moccasins, making walking harder than ever.

Rain fell all day and all night. They couldn't build a fire with wet wood, so they huddled under their sopping blankets and slept fitfully. By morning the rain had stopped and a warm sun greeted them. About noon they climbed a hill. Before them lay the valley of the Little Missouri River, a glistening emerald ribbon.

Pierre shot a big horn that afternoon, and a few hours later they made camp and ate, letting the horses graze. In the morning they crossed the Little Missouri and headed northeastward, crossing creeks that flowed north.

"I believe we're getting near the Yellowstone," Jed said, "because it's north of us and these creeks must be flowing into it."

Two days later they followed a small stream to the Yellowstone River, and after two more days they reached the junction of the Yellowstone and Missouri rivers.

As the two men approached Fort Henry, its gate swung open to the tired travelers.

"Where's Ashley?" everyone asked as Jed and Pierre swung off their horses. "Isn't he coming?"

As Jed told the story of the fight with the Rees, Major Henry paced the ground. "I've lost four men to the Blackfeet myself. There's got to be beaver in safer places. . . . Well, we've got to help General Ashley," he said. "Jed, you and Pierre will go back with me. We'll start in the morning. Now you'd better eat and have a drink before going to bed."

"I can sure stand something to eat. You got any hot coffee?"

"Coffee?" An amused look played on the major's face. "You've been in these mountains a year and you still don't drink anything stronger than coffee?" He laughed.

"He still have second thoughts about killing Indian, too," said Pierre.

The major eyed Jed. "Well, never mind. Come along. Let's try some roast buffalo rib, Jed. . . . I haven't heard grace over a meal for some time."

11

Grizzly Attack

It was early July before Jed returned downriver with Henry and his party of forty to fifty trappers. To their surprise, the Rees made no trouble as the canoes swept past to join Ashley in his camp below the mouth of the Cheyenne River.

General Ashley had sent the wounded and unwilling down the Missouri in one of the keelboats with a message to Fort Atkinson, the nearest military post. If the river was to be safe for fur companies, Ashley had said, the Rees must be punished. Now he was waiting for the promised troops.

Late in July, two hundred fifty soldiers of the Sixth Missouri Regiment arrived with Colonel Henry Leavenworth in command. Jedediah Smith, as leader of a band of trappers, marched up the river to help the soldiers. Though the battle was short, it settled very little. The Rees promised safer passage for fur trappers, but slipped away in the night, abandoning their villages. It did not seem to be a good sign. The business partners decided that Ashley would return to St. Louis to deal with company losses—more than four thousand dollars—and Henry and his trappers would take the necessary supplies overland to Fort Henry.

"Maybe we should not try to hold a fort near the Yellowstone and other points east of the Rockies," General Ashley suggested. "Instead we could send out small parties of trappers west of the mountains."

Major Henry agreed. There were fewer Indians inland

and they would not meet as many trappers hired by rival fur companies. From this central rendezvous point the trappers could turn in their furs and get supplies for another trapping season. Each summer all their trappers would meet at a central rendezvous and collect the peltries, which would be taken to St. Louis and shipped back East. "I have discussed the idea with Jim Clyman," Ashley said. "He thinks it would work." In fact, the idea would revolutionize the trading business, for the meeting site would be changed according to the movement of the trappers instead of requiring the trappers, traders, and Indians to come to the fixed site of a fort, or trading post.

"Let's send out two parties to start with," suggested Henry. "Jed Smith, Jim Clyman, and a dozen more men can take the Powder River country. I'll put you in charge, Jed. You've proven yourself—Captain."

"Thank you, sir."

"Fitzpatrick, you're second in command. I'll take the rest to the Yellowstone. We'll rejoin the twenty trappers I left at the fort later."

While Ashley left for St. Louis for more supplies, the trapping parties began their work. From then on, Jed was known as Captain Smith.

Some weeks later, Jed rode at the head of a band of fifteen trappers along the wooded slope east of the Powder River. Besides Thomas Fitzpatrick, the group included Jim Clyman, Big Art Black, and William Sublette.

Jed had convinced Tom Fitzpatrick it would be a good idea to split the party into two bands. Tom would lead one band and Jed the other.

"Smaller bands get better results," Jed said. "And seven or eight men make less noise than fifteen."

Two days after leaving Tom Fitzpatrick, Jed's men reached the Powder River, struggling through gray gullies in a misting rain. As Jed skirted a pine-covered ravine, his horse gave a frightened snort and bolted.

Seconds later, a huge grizzly bear barreled into his horse, knocking Jed from the saddle. As he hit the ground, he

snatched his knife. The grizzly lunged across the horse's body and flung out a heavy paw, claws extended. Jed felt a burning pain in his side. Ducking, he jabbed his knife into the animal. Then he found himself looking squarely into a cavernous mouth. As Jed twisted away, the grizzly's jaws closed down on the top of his head, ripping off part of his scalp.

Blinded by blood, Jed swung his knife at the bear. He slid to his knees and gasped in pain. Somewhere behind him he heard Art Black's deep voice:

"Ease off, Jed. You can't kill the grizzly any deader."

For a moment the trappers were immobilized by the gory sight. The bear had taken Jed's head in its mouth, clawing near an eye on one side. The ear on the other side was torn from his head.

"We gotta do something!" Art suddenly boomed.

He leaned over Jed. "Call it, Captain."

"Go for . . . water," Jed said in a ragged voice. Then he turned to Jim Clyman. "There's needle and thread in my possibles bag. You sew up the wounds, Jim."

"You want some whiskey to deaden the pain?" Art asked. "This time—"

"No. Jim's gentle with a needle," Jed said, gritting his teeth while Jim stitched the scalp back in place.

After Jim had finished with the scalp, Jed said, "What about my ear, Jim?"

"I can't do anything about your ear, Jed."

"Oh, yes, you can. At least, you've got to try."

Jim Clyman laid the torn ear to the head, stitching over and over. When the bloody job was done, he washed the wounds with fresh water. Then he snipped off what remained of Jed's buckskin shirt. Jed had four broken ribs. Taking a strip of buckskin, Jim fastened it snugly around Jed's body.

The men helped Jed onto his horse. They found a campsite and placed Jed in a tent, making him as comfortable as possible. Jim treated the wounds with soap and sugar. As

Jed lay on his blanket that night he read his Bible, thankful to be alive.

The trappers knew Jed's recovery would be slow, so they decided two men would stay with him while the rest went downriver to trap. They would return in about two weeks.

Several days later, after Jed's two companions had gone upstream to set traps, Jed heard wild cries. He was sure Indians had surprised them. Seizing his rifle and powder horn, he dragged himself into nearby bushes and waited. Soon he heard splashing from upstream; it was drawing nearer. A dozen Indians in war paint were cantering along the creek on their ponies. Seeing the empty camp and three horses, they helped themselves. Then with a yell, the Indians leaped on their mounts and galloped off downstream. As they rode away, two of the braves suddenly let out cries and brandished aloft two fresh scalps.

The evening air grew chill. Weak and sick, Jed began the long night alone. He crawled painfully out of his hiding place and after much effort gathered a pile of twigs and built a fire. By the flickering flames he paged through his Bible with shaky fingers, pausing at Job 33: "He is chastened also with pain upon his bed, and the multitude of his bones with strong pain. ... He shall return to the days of his youth. He shall pray unto God, and he will be favorable to him." *Dear God,* Jed prayed, *please don't forsake me!* Then he fell into an uneasy sleep.

When he awoke the next morning he dragged himself to the river to check on the traps, for he was out of food. The first was empty. He paused to pray for strength, and crawling to the next trap, he found a beaver. With his knife he skinned it and dragged it back to camp, where he cooked it over the fire and ate.

The next day he swallowed the last bite. Since he was too weak to set any traps, he faced being without food. For three days he had nothing to eat, lying helplessly on the ground. Again he looked to his Bible for courage.

"I will lift up mine eyes unto the hills from whence cometh my help." The words soothed him as he looked at the distant hills, and he prayed again. "Lord, where will I find help? I need help, Lord . . . food . . . My help cometh from the Lord," he added hoarsely.

Then he heard a faint rustle. A buck stood in the middle of a nearby clearing. Carefully he picked up his gun and shot. The deer crumpled.

Skinning the deer was hard, for Jed's head and body throbbed from the deep gashes and broken ribs. Finally he cut enough meat to roast over the fire.

Time dragged on. When would the trapping party return?

Jed crawled up a hill and looked around. All he could see was a valley slashed with creeks and furred with trees and brush. The far distant mountains were a purple blur against the horizon.

Not having strength to dry the deer meat, Jed had to watch it spoil after a few days. As crows picked the bones clean, Jed and wondered how long it would be until they would pick his bones.

Two more days Jed waited. He thought of his family back in Ashtabula. How long had it been since he had seen them? A year? Two? Would they ever meet again? He had hoped to earn money to help his brothers get an education. Fitfully he would scratch at the ground with a twig, mapping the area. His strength would not allow him any serious map-making.

Another two days dragged by without food. The pages of his Bible fell open to a familiar place: "The Lord is my shepherd. I shall not want . . . he maketh me to lie down in green pastures . . . He leadeth me beside still waters. He restoreth my soul. Yea, though I walk through the valley of the shadow of death, I will fear no evil *for thou art with me.*"

Was this his "valley of the shadow"? As he prayed, a quiet peace filled his heart, and he knew he was ready to meet his God.

The next morning Jed heard the sound of horses hooves on stone—shod horses. He started to sit up quickly and winced. Slowly he cocked his rifle.

A tall man with a party of three rode into camp. "I am Colonel Keemle of the Missouri Fur Company," the man said, "and I'm looking for Tom Fitzpatrick. Who are you, and what's happened to you?"

Jed released the hammer on his rifle and quietly told them what had happened. The colonel offered to take him to the rest of his trappers.

As Jed was helped onto a horse he was glad he hadn't had to move any sooner. It had been less than two weeks since he was mauled by the grizzly.

Traveling west, Keemle's party met Tom Fitzpatrick a few days later. Now Jed would soon join the Ashley-Henry Company again.

It would be a good time to pause and praise the Lord.

12

Learning an Indian Secret

The days grew colder as November winds howled. Frost laced the prairies and a thin layer of ice covered the ravines. Jed and his band moved west, hoping to reach the camps of the Crow Indians on the Wind River before winter set in.

The Crows were friendly to trappers. They raised fine horses, and Jed needed horses. The Crows were also much cleaner than most Indians he had seen.

The trappers met roving bands of Cheyenne along the way and all of them were friendly. Sometimes a few Cheyenne rode with them for a day or two to trade horses for gewgaws.

Food was scarce and Jed was in a hurry to get to the Crows. As he rode ahead he sang lustily.

> "O for a thousand tongues to sing
> My great Redeemer's praise,
> The glories of my God and King,
> The triumphs of His grace!"

"Is that Jed a'hollerin' up ahead?" Art Black asked Jim Clyman.

"Yep . . . and nope. That ain't no hollerin'. If you'd of been in church more often when you was growin' up, you might of recognized it was a hymn. . . . He says singin' 'em out is a help to him."

"I'll be dogged if that Jed Smith ain't the oddest critter I ever saw," Art said with a big laugh. "He even shaves out here."

"May be—but I've never seen a better mountain man," Jim said.

Cold and hungry, the men finally reached the Crow camp just as snowflakes were falling.

That night Jed was invited to the chief's tepee, where warriors passed the peace pipe. Cutnose, one warrior, spoke enough English for Jed to understand.

"Chief wants to know if you have brought whiskey to trade," Cutnose said after the pipe had made its rounds.

Jed looked at the circle of warriors. He didn't want to hurt their feelings and he didn't want to anger them either. Still, he always spoke to an Indian with a "straight tongue." Although he didn't approve of his own men drinking, he let it pass as long as they behaved. Whiskey seemed to be a part of a trapper's life.

Now he looked calmly at the chief before replying. "Tell him no. We have no firewater for our red brothers. We give no poison to our friends."

As Cutnose repeated the message, Jed watched the chief's face. A smile lit up the craggy bronze features. He spoke calmly to the interpreter.

"He says, 'The white chief is young in years but old in wisdom,' " Cutnose said. "He does not want any poison water among his people. He also says you are welcome to stay among the Crows."

Jed was pleased with the chief's answers. Good relationships were important. Sometimes they meant the difference between life and death for trappers.

The next day Jed's men joined the Crows in a buffalo hunt, for great herds were massed in the valleys. The best Crow Indians and Jed's sharpest shooters were stationed along the two ridges overlooking a narrow canyon. The fastest riders rode into the valleys where the buffalo grazed. As riders came upon the herd—shouting, waving blankets, shooting guns—the frightened animals thundered into the canyon, hooves pounding. From the ridges rifles cracked and arrows zinged. They dropped a thousand buffalo in two days.

Immediately Crow women, children, and old men went to work butchering the fallen animals. They cut off juicy steaks from ribs and roasted them over the fire for a feast that night. After everyone had eaten, the men sat and smoked while the women cut the rest of the meat into long thin strips for winter jerky. Jed watched, wondering if their method might be any different from Jim Clyman's.

As long as the weather permitted, Jed's men set their beaver traps. Winter would soon close in. After their traps were set they quickly built shanties of cottonwoods and buffalo skins near the Indian settlements. The Crows seemed happy to have them as their guests, for when Jed's trappers brought in beaver and skinned them, they gave the meat to the Indians.

Soon the heavy snows began, coming in the teeth of howling northwinds. The trappers learned that the Wind River did not get its name for nothing: Icy blasts screamed as snow piled high around the skin tepees. But inside they were snug and warm.

Some of Jed's men joined the Crows in their camps, smoking with the braves or flirting with the maidens, wrestling or riding. Among themselves, besides eating and sleeping a lot, the trappers sang, clogged to an old fiddle, or swapped tall tales. Jed would write in his journals, and read from his book about Lewis and Clark as well as from his Bible. Sometimes he would be requested to read aloud, which he was glad to oblige.

Often he grew restless. There were too many white spaces on the map, and growing fat and lazy wasn't filling them. He'd heard Cutnose mention a pass through the Shining Mountains and he craved to find it. He had also heard that here the rivers divided, that water on the east side of this high ridge flowed into the Mississippi River and went down to the Gulf of Mexico. All the water on the west side ran from the Rockies into the Gulf of California and the Pacific Ocean. From the East they flowed into the Atlantic and from the West into the Pacific. This was called the Great Divide.

"I know there's a lot of country ahead of us," Jed told Tom Fitzpatrick, Billy Sublette, and Davey Jackson as the four men made plans for travel. "We must find out what it's like. I guess I'll not be satisfied until I find that Great Divide."

"It could be a long ways off," said Tom.

"And it's a God-forsaken country out there, if you ask me," put in Davey. "Do you think Hudson's Bay trappers have been this far south?"

"Possible. I hear they take beaver wherever they can find it," said Tom.

"Like us," added Billy with a laugh.

"We have as much right in these parts as they do," said Tom.

"I'd say more!" said Billy, growing serious.

"No need of locking horns if we don't need to," said Jed.

"I know I'd just as soon stay out of their way," muttered Davey. "I hear they're a mean bunch."

"I wonder just how much the Crows do know about going direct over the mountains?" said Tom.

Jed believed they could cross the Shining Mountains—but where? Maybe the Crows could tell them.

Yet no matter how hard Jed tried, he couldn't make Cutnose understand. Finally he had an idea. He spread a buffalo robe on the floor of the tepee, skin side up. Then he heaped up sand and rocks on it to indicate valleys and mountains.

"How do you get across?" he asked.

Suddenly the braves began to talk among themselves with what seemed like some alarm. They looked at their chief. Slowly he nodded. Quickly they moved some rocks and placed sand to make almost level land, then ridges for mountains. Then they walked with their fingers over the crest and down the other side. From this Jed understood this crossing was in a *southwest* direction from the Crow camp. That's what he had wanted to find out.

"No white man know of crossing," Cutnose added.

The trappers produced gewgaws. It was an occasion.

Jed itched to get going. In February, as soon as the first snows had melted, he and his fifteen trappers told the Crows good-bye and rode out of the camp with their pelts and pack horses. If they followed the Sweetwater River, the Crows had said, they would find the pass through the mountains. The weather was still bitterly cold, but Jed had waited as long as he could. He had to discover what lay beyond the Rockies.

A blizzard blew out of the north as they approached the mountain range. In a sheltered place under a shelving rock they waited out the storm. Now they were on the banks of the Sweetwater.

They would cache their pelts in the Sweetwater valley, Jed and Jim decided. They had brought their whole store of furs on pack horses. Moving across the mountains was hard enough with supplies; it was best to cache the furs. They could pick them up before the next rendezvous.

"First thing you do when you make a cache," Jim said, "is to make sure no Indians are around."

After checking, he ordered the men to dig a large hole in the ground; then he told them to tunnel back into the ground for several yards. He showed them how to line the tunnel with brush and grass. Then Jim, Jed, and Art packed the furs and all the goods they didn't need into the tunnel. They filled the hole leading down to the tunnel with dirt, after which all signs of digging had to be wiped out. As a last rite, Jim scattered the ashes of their campfire over the opening. "No one should be able to find that."

Art Black muttered, "Just so *we* don't forget where it's at."

Jed and Art watched as Jim went to a tree that seemed to have grown out from under a boulder and marked its trunk: three spots and a stripe.

They promised each other that if they were separated, they would meet here in June.

Now they moved on. Jed and his men pushed westward, following the Sweetwater River into the wide valley that led up the mountains. It slanted so gradually they hardly realized they were climbing.

Now and then Jed tossed a stick into the water. Always it floated east, back the way they had come. "When a stick floats west, we have found the Indian pass to the other side of the Shining Mountains," Jed told Moses "Black" Harris.

For six days the little party pushed across the plateaus. At one point they crossed a dry rolling highland and the waterhole they had anticipated was dry. Suffering from exhaustion as well as thirst, the men scattered in hopes of finding water. Some of them faltered and two collapsed. When Jim Clyman found what they were all so desperate for, signalling to the others with a shot, Jed carried water back to the two who could summon no energy to continue.

Four days they were without food, and Jed grew worried. Had they taken the wrong turn? Were they really headed for the pass? Had Cutnose told them the truth?

As they continued, they encountered packed snow and freezing cold. For fifteen days they melted snow to drink. As they climbed higher, Jed was sure they were approaching the crest of the divide.

One afternoon in late February as the trappers camped beside a mountain spring, Jed took a walk along the stream. Pausing, he picked up a twig and dropped it into the water. Then he raised his hand as if in silent praise.

"He's found it!" Tom told Davey, and the two hurried to join Jed.

"We're over!" Jed yelled and he fired his rifle, its echo answering from the low hills.

The men came running and jumping up the stream's bank, throwing in sticks and shouting as they floated west. The men had finally reached the Great Divide!

It was not the steep winding crevice through towering mountains that they had expected. It was instead a broad treeless valley of grass twenty to thirty miles wide. *This was it, the South Pass!*

"It's a great day," Jed told Tom solemnly, "and worth the long trek, the hunger and thirst of these past weeks. Here wagons will someday cross the mountains to a new home in the West!"

In fact, besides inviting more trappers, the pass would open the way for pioneers bound for Oregon, prospectors bound for California, and missionaries bound for both. (But it would be the likes of Moses "Black" Harris and Tom Fitzpatrick—not Jed—who would lead them.)

Jed and his trappers found many beavers on the western side of the Divide, but trapping didn't interest Jed the way it once had. He had begun to fill in the white spaces on the map!

13

A Surprise among the Flatheads

A busy year of trapping had passed, and it was time for the rendezvous. By June 18, 1825, Jed and his men had returned with their pelts to the agreed upon meeting spot, Henry's Fork on the Green River (near Flaming Gorge Dam in northeastern Utah).

Major Henry eyed Jed's scarred face and shook his head. "Boy, that didn't happen to you shaving. What happened?"

Jed told him about the fight with the grizzly, saying he was grateful to God that he had survived.

"Well, I'm glad you pulled through too. You're stuff good mountain men are made of. . . . As for me, I've had enough of the trapping life, fighting Blackfeet, and rough country. I'm ready to retire to St. Louis. How'd you like to be General Ashley's partner?"

A nice birthday present, thought Jed. *Ashley & Smith Fur Company.* He would be twenty-seven that month.

When Jed had arrived at the rendezvous he had found more than six hundred trappers and Indians camped along the Green. It was almost like a state fair or carnival, only wilder. Ashley had brought a large supply of trade goods from St. Louis and was doing a heavy business. Sugar, coffee, tobacco, powder, bullets, rifles, blankets, kettles, whiskey, and all sorts of gewgaws were exchanged for piles of fur and buffalo robes.

Snake and Ute Indians, Canadians, Easterners, mountaineers—men from everywhere, it seemed—had gathered to trade, drink, and sing. There were also contests of every kind: jumping, roping, shooting, horse racing. At night trappers and Indians joined in a wild dance around the camp-fires.

When the rendezvous ended, Ashley had collected huge piles of furs to ship to St. Louis. Jim Clyman and fifty men would go with him. Jed would miss Jim. The gray mountain man had been a good friend and had taught him much of what he knew about Indians, trapping, and surviving. He owed a great deal to Jim Clyman.

From the rendezvous, Jed's party of six men moved swiftly north, toward the headwaters of the Columbia, for the fall hunt, trapping beaver as they went from stream to stream. Through forests and over high mountains they pushed, collecting some nine hundred beaver skins.

Along the banks of the Snake River, Jed ran into a party of British trappers. The Hudson's Bay Company was the largest trapping company based in Canada, and its trappers had come if not into American territory at least into disputed territory. Their leader, Captain Alexander Ross, was not happy to see Jed, since the two fur companies were rivals.

In December, Jed followed a large party of southbound Canadian trappers. Their leader, Peter Skene Ogden, had been ordered by the Hudson's Bay Company to clear all the beaver from the streams on the Snake Plain. The British knew that once the boundary dispute between Canada and the United States was settled, all the lands south of the Columbia would most likely belong to the United States. So it was smart to get all the furs they could before the Americans moved in.

Jed quickly caught on to their scheme and decided to get ahead of Ogden's party. The trappers hurried back to the Snake River. Jed wondered if it was true about the Hudson's Bay trappers being a mean bunch.

From here, both groups moved on southward to the Cache Valley on the Bear River. Jed wanted to learn all the tricks of the trade from the British trappers, so he tagged after them. Although Ross didn't like the idea, he decided to accept the presence of Jed's trappers as added insurance against Indian attack.

Ross took the Americans with him to the Flathead Post to trade for goods. The Flathead Indians met them in Bitterroot Valley (in what is now northwest Montana). Jed was impressed with these Indians. They were slender, well-built, and looked groomed and clean.

When they sat down to eat with their white visitors, the Flatheads bowed their heads and asked the blessing on their meat.

Jed stared. Immediately after the prayer he asked, "Who is your leader?" After being answered, he fired another question: "You pray before your meals, who are you praying to?"

"We worship the same God as the white man," Chief Big Ignace said. "We believe in a Father, Creator of heaven and earth and of all things in heaven and earth. We believe He sent His only Son to die for the sins of men, and that men nailed this Son to a tree. But on the third day He arose from the dead and walked among his friends."

His face alive with interest, Jed interrupted. "And He went back to heaven—"

"Where He sits at the right hand of God," said Big Ignace. "And He will come again to judge all men, red or white."

"Just as it says in the Heavenly Book," said Jed as he drew his Bible from his possibles bag.

"*You* have the Book?" asked Big Ignace. It was his turn to become animated. "Will you teach us more?"

"I will be glad to tell you what I know."

The chief told Jed that Christian Iroquois Indians from Canada had come among the Flathead and Nez Perce Indians and intermarried, bringing the gospel with them.

Jed learned that they also believed that a man must have only one wife, to whom he must be true until death. They must not steal or lie, and neither were they to speak poorly of others.

That night Jed and the chiefs conducted a service around

the campfire, sharing their faith in Jesus Christ. As the smoke of the fire curled upward, the sound of Christian hymns rose above the barking dogs and neighing horses. This time Jed was not singing alone. Having been brought up in a Christian home, he felt it had been too long since he had worshiped with other believers.

"And where can we find a Heavenly Book like yours to tell us more about our God?" Big Ignace asked.

Jed knew of a Methodist church in St. Louis. Perhaps that was the place to ask.

Records show that in 1832, five delegates from the Nez Perces—Flatheads or Iroquois—came to St. Louis to ask more about the Heavenly Book.

News appeared in the March 1833 issue of the *Christian Advocate:*

> Hear! hear! Who will respond to the call beyond the Rocky Mountains and tell the people about Jesus Christ? Bright will be his crown, glorious his reward!

By June, Jason Lee was appointed superintendent of the New Oregon Mission. In August his nephew, Rev. Daniel Lee, joined him. Thus Protestant missions were begun among the Indians of the Northwest in the 1830s.

Visited in 1834, the Nez Perces and Flatheads were described by Captain Benjamin Bonneville as being "friendly and honest to the greatest degree in their dealings with the white men. Their honesty is pure and their purity and practicing the rites of their religion is most remarkable. They are certainly more like a nation of saints than a horde of savages."

In the lonely wilderness Jedediah Smith had found unexpected Christian fellowship. It awakened in him a continuing need. Later he would write to his parents:

"God only knows I feel the need of the Christian Church. I hope you remember me before the Throne of Grace!"

14

Beyond the Shining Mountains

Five days before Christmas, Peter Skene Ogden decided to move south. Jed's party went with him. They pushed through mountains thickly timbered with pine and spruce, crossed swollen streams, and finally reached the Salmon River.

Here Jed said good-bye and set out with his own party, heading still farther south. Snow lay deep on the high plateaus, and it took nearly a month to reach the Snake River.

Late that winter Jed led his party of trappers around the north end of Salt Lake and across the mountains toward the West. Looking for water to drink, they found only a few salty springs. The salt desert produced almost no grass for the horses. And there wasn't a beaver in sight.

Jed gave up and turned north to the Snake Plain for spring trapping. Working northwest, they trapped the Boise River.

Thus a busy year of trapping had passed. Spring meant that the time for the rendezvous in Cache Valley was drawing near. It was at this rendezvous of 1826 that Ashley called Jed to his tent. Billy Sublette and Davey Jackson were there, too.

"Jed," said General Ashley, "like Major Henry, I too have decided to sell out. If you men are interested, you can buy my share of the company. By your work—and the work of all the others—I have become a man of means. I thank you all. My plan is to take up my abode in St. Louis, where

everyone of you are welcome anytime. . . . Now, I understand Billy and Davey want to join you as partners."

After signing the necessary papers, the new company of
fur trappers—Smith, Sublette, and Jackson—had bought
the firm for thirty thousand dollars. Billy Sublette would
be the businessman, buying and selling; Davey Jackson
would direct the trapping parties; and Jedediah Smith would
search for new beaver country. The first two smiled a bit,
for they knew this would give Jed a chance to explore and
to work on his maps.

"Let's carry on the way General Ashley did," Billy Sublette suggested. "With a rendezvous each summer we'll take
in all the furs the free trappers and Indians bring us."

"We'll seek new territory for trapping," Jed put in.

"You'll find it, if anyone will," Davey mused.

Jed went back to study his maps again. Beyond the Great
Salt Lake was unknown country, and he had to plan his
route carefully.

For the next few days Jed busily packed for the Southwest
expedition. Besides traps, provisions, and ammunition, the
expedition would take gewgaws (ribbons, rings, combs, bells)
and trade goods (lead, awls, butcher knives, arrow points)
for the Indians. A chest contained important papers such
as contracts, company books, Jed's journals and those of his
second in command, Harrison Rogers.

Rogers was company clerk and keeper of accounts, as Jed
had been for Ashley. Jed then became "booshway," or leader,
to the men, and Harrison Rogers "little booshway." Rogers
identified himself as a Christian, which Jed welcomed. It
was good to know someone else looked to God for help.
Maybe that's why Jed chose Rogers as second in command.

Jed reviewed his sketchy knowledge of medicine, since
there was no doctor in the party. For rattlesnake bites and
other small open wounds, stopping the bleeding and dis-
infecting the wound was achieved by burning a pinch of
gunpowder (this was known as "red-eye") in it; salve for
lacerations was made up of soap and sugar or beaver's oil
(castoreum). Liver pills were made from calomel, and tar

drops were good for colds and sore throats. "Bitters" was made from water and buffalo gall, serving to aid in digestion and pacify the stomach generally.

Art Black and Billy Sublette watched Jed check his list of supplies. "You're headin' into unknown country," Billy told him, "and your chances of coming back aren't good, you know."

"If I do what is right, the Lord will give me strength to do it," Jed said, poising his quill pen over his checklist.

"Men have been right before and didn't manage to do what they wanted," Art growled.

"For me," Jed said quietly, "to die in faith is to die trying— just like those people in Hebrews 11: 'not having received the promises, but having seen them afar off.' "

When Jed left, Billy shook his head. "I don't get it with his religious talk. Yet sometimes I wish I was going with him. Something about him makes you feel good."

At twenty-eight years of age, Jedediah Smith, "a mild man and a Christian," was chief commander of three hundred mountaineers, among whom very few were mild or religious. A ragged scar ran down his face, raising one eyebrow like a question mark. But there was no question in his mind. He knew exactly what he wanted to do.

Jed asked for volunteers for this trip into the unknown, and seventeen men responded. Included in the party were Abraham LaPlant, who spoke a little Spanish, Martin McCoy, John Gaither, Peter Ranne, a black man, Louis Pombert, Silas Gobel and James Reed, blacksmiths, and Robert Evans. Besides blacksmiths, in this group were good hunters and horsemen as well.

On Tuesday, August 22, 1826, Jed and his party struck out on the Southwest expedition. He chose to go past the Great Salt Lake into a dry, drab country, leaving the high peaks of the Rockies, skirting what is now Zion National Park. Before them lay wilderness, including the white sands of Southern California's Mojave Desert.

Jed, a blue bandanna tied around his brown head, rode

eagerly ahead, looking for a route by which they could make their way. Harrison Rogers brought up the rear.

Jed led them through present-day sites of Utah: Brigham, Ogden, Salt Lake City, Provo, Spanish Fork, Payson, Nephi. They followed the Sevier River (which Jed named Ashley) to the mountains that separate the Great Basin from tributaries of the lower Colorado River.

Day after day blinding salt-covered flats stretched out before them. The grueling ride in this desolate country soon began to wear on the men.

"Hey, Captain Smith," Pombert growled, "we came to trap beaver, not to cross no-man's land."

Other men grumbled. "Where's Jed think he's takin' us? There's nothing down here."

But Jed kept them moving. He was looking for beaver, determined to go where no Americans had gone before.

As the bright September sun blazed down on them, rivers turned to mere trickles. There was almost no grass, and soon horses and mules began to falter and drop.

The men grew more gloomy each day. They rode through deep dark passes and dry plains. Once in awhile their route led to a ridge from which they could see strange towers of rock glinting in the sun. Jed always rode ahead, searching the best route to follow, his sharp blue eyes on the horizon. He looked for Indian signs, studying them when he found them.

At night the men sat around the campfire without their usual jokes and tall tales. As was his custom, Jed read his Bible and wrote in his journal.

"What's he after?" James Reed groused one evening when another day had dragged by without grass or water.

"Captain's playin' with death," Pombert muttered. "What's out there that we have to see? Ain't no beaver in them dry streams."

More horses and mules died without water as the party moved south. The men, in desperation, ate the tasteless, leather-like meat of the horses. When they had started, there were fifty animals; by the time they reached the Colorado River only twenty-eight were left. These were heavily loaded, staggering up sharp mountain curves and carrying the loads of pack animals that had already dropped. If they didn't find grass and water soon, all the animals would die, and the lives of the men would be in jeopardy as well. The land was barren and desolate, with nothing ahead but sand and sagebrush.

One day several of the men approached Jed. "Why don't we turn back? We'll all die out here if nothing comes up soon."

"It would be more dangerous to turn back now than to keep going," Jed said. "We'll find food for ourselves and the horses sooner by moving south. I'm sure we'll find an Indian village in a few days."

Jed was right. Emerging from the Black Mountains two days later, the starving men stumbled into a broad valley graced with green willows and mesquite; the scrubby mesquite tree was an especially welcome sight, having a pod that served well as feed for livestock. Near the Colorado River they came upon an Indian village made of mud houses, snuggling in the lush green valley.

"I'll be dogged if I know how Jed knew we'd find them!" said Silas Gobel, one of the blacksmiths. "But I know he's got faith in himself and his God."

"He's got a feeling about the land too, wherever he goes," added Robert Evans. "I know Jed Smith is one leader I want to follow."

The Indians living in the village approached them, waving their bows and arrows in greeting it seemed. The men wore little more than loincloths and the women wore what appeared to be skirts of bark. Jed went to meet them, giving the Indian sign of peace. They were Mojaves, they made Jed understand, and their hearts were good.

Although the Mojaves were friendly, Jed warned his men always to be on guard. "The Indians probably won't cause problems if we treat them right," he said. "But I'll whip the first one of you who causes trouble." He knew how important good relationships with the Indians were.

For two weeks the half-starved trappers feasted on pumpkins, beans, fish, melons, and corn from the Mojaves' storehouses. The horses grew fat on the grass, mesquite pod, and water of the valley, being in good shape by the time the trappers were ready to move on.

Jed traded for more horses and then asked for them and the supplies to be ferried across the river. With a Spanish-speaking half-breed named Francisco and another Indian guide to lead the way, they headed directly toward the white-hot sands of the Mojave Desert.

Jed was sure they weren't too far from some of the California missions. But both Francisco and his companion warned Jed he was going into dangerous territory. The trappers soon discovered it was even worse than the country they had just crossed.

"I thought we'd already been through the fiery furnace," one of the men grumbled, "but I was wrong!"

Yet there was no turning back. The men knew Jed Smith wouldn't go back, even if he could. The search for beaver, the yen to explore, the belief that what lay ahead couldn't be as bad as what lay behind, led him on.

What lay ahead, however, was more desert land of cactus and yucca, its stiff, sword-like leaves forming a fierce pin cushion below its greenish-white flowers. For a day they stumbled over miles of glistening white salt. Day after scorching day passed. Mirages mocked them as they traveled on without finding water. Sometimes the heat was unbearable, and Jed hit upon the idea of having the men dig into the sand until they found cool earth and lay in it.

When things got rough Jed burst into one of his hymns. Somehow it strengthened him.

> "Meet and right it is to sing,
> In every time and place,
> Glory to our Heavenly King,
> The God of truth and grace."

Jed found a curious river; it seemed to duck under the

sand for miles at a stretch, popping up now and again. He called it the Inconstant (since called the Mojave). When water was scarce, he told the men to prick the cactus and suck its juice. This helped to quench their thirst and keep them going. But without good food and water they grew thin and deeply discouraged.

Though it was November, the desert continued to exact its toll for crossing: Throats parched and strength fading they stumbled on for two more weeks. How long would the exhausting trek continue?

One day later, when the weary trappers could scarcely drag themselves, their Indian guides pointed south to a gap in the San Bernardino Mountains.

"Come on, men!" Jed cried. "When we get through that gap we'll find food and water."

Jed called it the Gap of the Mountain; it was the gateway between the desert and the coastal plain and came to be called the Cajon Pass.

The trail led up a cool, pine-grown ridge so steep that they had to help each other up. Dragging his heavily loaded mule by a lead rope, one of the men muttered: "I don't know how you do it, Cap'n, but if you can keep goin' so can I."

After an agonizing climb, they reached the trail's summit. The men threw themselves on the hard earth. Rough as they were, they felt like offering a prayer of thanks. As Jed looked down into the green valley below, he bowed and thanked God for bringing them through the hot desert and treacherous mountains. They had completed a journey of seven hundred miles.

Fresh, sparkling water tumbled through the rich green valley and large herds of cattle and horses grazed peacefully in the meadows. To the north lay a range of bold, rough mountains; to the south stretched a line of low, rolling hills.

"Is it Eden?" asked a hoarse voice.

"If it ain't, it'll do," someone answered.

The ragged, half-starved trappers scrambled down the trail to drink their fill of water. Jed's tired blue eyes traveled westward through the clear November air, following the pointing finger of one of the Indian guides.

"San Gabriel," Francisco said, indicating that somewhere in the area of the fertile valley was a Spanish settlement.

Jed stared far, far out. There, beneath the sun, lay a shimmering band of blue.

"The Pacific," Jed whispered, as if he might have entered a church.

"The Pacific!" The men shouted, jerking off their tattered caps and throwing them into the air.

At last they had reached the Province of California.

15

"I Am Not a Spy!"

As the ragged band of starving trappers rode down the San Bernardino Valley, an Indian native of the valley galloped ahead to the San Gabriel Mission to tell Father Joseph Sanchez that a group of Americans had struggled across the mountains through Cajon Pass to the green valley belonging to the mission.

The little party of trappers rode through great herds of cattle, sheep, and horses, finally camping among a stand of live oaks. The Indian messenger returned, along with Spanish soldiers riding on gaily decorated horses. All were polite and kind, especially when they saw the burnt faces and gaunt bodies in their tattered outfits.

The Indians spoke a few words to nearby herdsmen, who butchered a cow and roasted it over an open fire. That night the battered band wolfed down steaks and cornbread. Not since being among the Mojaves had Jed and his men looked upon such a contented group of people.

After being invited to the mission, Jed rode into San Gabriel with the military commandant, leaving Harrison Rogers in charge.

California had belonged to Spain and was now under Mexico, who had recently revolted from Spain. The Californios, as they were called, spoke mostly Spanish. Abraham LaPlant went with Jed as interpreter.

The San Gabriel Mission seemed very rich, for the Franciscan friars had tens of thousands of animals, with grazing lands stretching all the way to the Pacific Ocean. Jed learned that about twenty-five hundred Indians lived near the mission or in surrounding villages. In the mission complex were also huge orchards, vineyards, soap works, and weaving and sewing rooms.

"I would like to know about your country," Father Sanchez said while showing Jed around. "We have a curiosity about the land to the east. The ships with their captains have visited us, but coming overland—that is most unusual! You know," Father Sanchez chuckled, "at one time we believed our California was an island. . . . Of course, you must go to San Diego to report to the governor of our province, José María Echeandía, that you are here."

"I suppose I must," Jed said, "although I'd like to move on with my trappers as soon as I can."

The priest frowned. "I'm not sure how well the governor will receive you. You see, he does not look kindly upon outsiders. He, or perhaps Mexico, like Spain, is fearful of foreigners, who might have . . . designs on our country. And Senor Echeandía is new, only a year since he was sent from Mexico. But if you show him your papers permitting your travel . . ."

"We have no such papers," said Jed. "I wasn't sure how far I would get in my travels. I have no permission to trap here. Perhaps the governor will understand. I will write and ask to see him and explain."

"You and your men may stay here at the mission until you are summoned to San Diego," Father Sanchez replied kindly. "But let me warn you. The governor is a strict man."

While little children gazed at the bearded, long-haired strangers, the missionary fathers asked many questions. They had heard about the Great Salt Lake. What was the country like? What kind of people lived in the vast wilderness between California and St. Louis? What were the laws like in the American States?

Jed drew maps for them. He also told them of the Indians: the easy-going Snakes, the crafty Blackfeet, the friendly Crows, the unpredictable Mojaves.

95

The men of the mission readily accepted Jed, the "booshway," and Rogers, "little booshway." When Father Sanchez saw how ragged the trappers were, he gave Jed sixty-four yards of cloth so he and his men could make shirts for themselves. In response, Rogers made Father Sanchez a present of a buffalo robe. In return, the padre gave him a fine blanket.

Together with LaPlant, Jed went to the pueblo of Los Angeles where he met with Father Martinez to buy horses and mules for the journey to leave California.

One night at the supper table the priest asked Harrison Rogers about his religion.

"I was brought up under the doctrine that a man cannot forgive sins. Only God has that power," Rogers said quietly. "I confess my sins in prayer to God, not to a man."

With this response, Jedediah Smith heartily agreed.

Rogers wrote in his journal: "The missionaries and people of San Gabriel all appear friendly and treat us well. Although they are Catholic by profession, they allow us the liberty of our own beliefs and treat us as they treat their own countrymen and brethren."

Even so, some of Jed's men needed correction, particularly James Reed, who on one occasion entered the priests' dining hall in the middle of their mealtime and helped himself; he was drunk.

When Governor Echeandía received Jed's letter, he was worried. "It is all right for the *yanqui* to come to California in ships to trade," he muttered, "but now he sneaks in through the mountains behind our backs!"

"Couldn't you arrest them and put them on the American ships in the harbor?" his aide suggested.

"Perhaps I could. But then what happens? My government already has trouble with the American leaders in Washington. If this man Smith is important, Washington will become angry." He shrugged. "What can I do?"

By the time Jed had received his summons from the governor and arrived in San Diego, the governor was in a sullen mood.

"Why did you come to California? Why are you spying on us?" he demanded angrily.

"I am not a spy," Jed said. "My men are trappers. We were searching for beaver but lost most of our horses in the dry Mojave Desert. We were forced to push on across the mountains or die."

"But you cannot stay!" the governor stormed. "You should be in jail. You have no papers, no permits to trap!"

"I don't plan to stay," Jed said politely. "All I need is your permission to move north toward Oregon and cross the mountains to my own country."

"That is not possible," Echeandía said coldly. He eyed the tall clean-shaven man with the scarred, question-mark eyebrow. Having been told that Jed had seventeen armed men at San Gabriel, the governor didn't want to get into a fight. But he couldn't allow these Americans to go north and see the thinly-populated country. This sharp-eyed *yanqui* would see too much. Before long, other Americans would flock to California.

"I only wish to leave your country peacefully," Jed said. "But I cannot risk the lives of my men by taking them back over the Mojave Desert—that's Starvation Country!"

"You will come back later. Then I will give you my answer," the Governor said, waving him out. He had to think of something.

After Jed left, he spoke to LaPlant. "I understand there are American ships at anchor in San Diego. I must see them as soon as possible." Jed was ready to accept any plan as long as he didn't have to return across the desert.

Almost three weeks later he stood before Echeandía again, hoping his appeal to the merchantmen had worked.

"I have a paper here," Governor Echeandía said, "signed by six of your countrymen. They have assured me they believe your story and that you are not a spy. But I cannot allow you to go toward Oregon. You must return by the same route you came. However, I will provide you with supplies so you can leave."

"But, Governor—"

97

"Do not argue," Governor Echeandía said. "I have done all I intend to do."

Jed returned to San Gabriel, troubled but determined. He could not deliberately endanger the lives of his men by leading them back the way they had come. If he went north for only a few hundred miles, surely he would be able to avoid the desert when he turned back east.

Before the men left, Father Sanchez prepared a farewell feast for Jed and Harrison Rogers. He gave them gifts of cheese, brandy, and blankets. He also handed Jed a paper with permission to take all the supplies he needed.

The evening before the trappers left, Harrison Rogers wrote in his diary:

"Old Father Sanchez has been the greatest friend that I ever met . . . in all my travels. He is worthy of being called a Christian, as he possesses charity in the highest degree and [is] a friend to the poor and distressed. I ever shall hold him as a man of God, taking us when in distress, feeding and clothing us. May God prosper him and all such men."

The little band left San Gabriel on Thursday, February 1, 1827. They crossed the San Bernardino Mountains through Cajon Pass and turned north—skirting the Mojave Desert.

No one bothered the trappers as they moved north into the San Joaquin Valley, toward the Stanislaus River, a branch of the San Joaquin River. Bounded on the west by the Coast Range and on the east by the Sierra Nevadas, the San Joaquin Valley was filled with a variety of wild animals and featured a varied geography. Beaver trapping along the Stanislaus was very good. Jed decided to camp there for the rest of the winter.

"We can't possibly move the pelts across the high mountains until we know where to go. I'm going to leave you and the beaver pelts here, with Harrison Rogers," Jed told the group when spring stippled the valley with green. "You will be trapping while I take Robert Evans and Silas Gobel with me to look for another way to go East. We'll be back in about four months. If we aren't back in six, don't wait."

"We'll wait for you," John Hanna said. "When you say you'll be back, we know you'll be back."

16

Death Stalks the Desert

On May 20, 1827, Jed Smith, Robert Evans, and Silas
Gobel started up the north fork of the Stanislaus River to
cross the Sierra Nevada mountain range, the whole of which
Jed named Mt. St. Joseph (after Father Sanchez, who had
treated them so kindly). Seven horses and two mules carried
hay for the animals and food for the men.

Choosing a canyon that looked promising, Jed led the way
up the mountains. Before long the little cavalcade began to
slip and slide on the snow, trying to keep from tumbling to
the rocky bottom of the gorges they found themselves in.
At night they slept in the snow, huddling together to keep
warm.

The climb took eight agonizing days. At one point, a horse
with its pack stepped too near the edge of a narrow ledge
and hurtled to its death. Later a mule, including its load,
vanished under the deep snow that blanketed their route.

But once the group arrived on the ridge of the range, the
snow was packed so tightly that the animals' hoofs sank
only through the crust, allowing better footing. As the three
men stumbled down the east side of the mountain range,
they were sure they had at last found a pass. Indeed they
had, Ebbetts Pass.

"That's enough to wind a mountain goat!" said Silas Gobel,
looking behind them at the awesome mountain range they
had just crossed.

Now they had scaled the mountains and were crossing

the foothills, but they faced a six-hundred mile trek to the Great Salt Lake. Ahead lay the sun-baked Nevada plains and what looked like endless rows of saw-toothed hills. They struck an easterly, rather than a northeasterly, direction, missing the Humboldt River (a route that would later be taken by Joseph Walker and again by John Fremont, among others). Before long they almost wished for snow again.

Occasionally they met a few pathetic Indians who lived on grass seed and grasshoppers. For weeks after leaving their party at the Stanislaus, they plodded through the sand until they reached the Deep Creek Mountains, near what is now the border of Nevada and Utah. His blue bandanna around his head, Jed rode at the head of the little caravan. The men's eyes ached from the heat and their throats burned with thirst.

The hot winds swept stinging salt into their faces and the shifting sand dragged at their feet. Every step was painful. Four of their remaining horses died as they struggled over the treacherous desert.

Jed searched the horizon anxiously. "I think we're on the south side of the Great Salt Lake," he said hopefully. "Before long we'll reach Bear Lake for the rendezvous."

But he was wrong. The endless scorching heat and stinging sand dogged them day after agonizing day. Now and then an antelope bounded into view in the distance, but the men were too weak to chase it down. Jed shot a few jackrabbits, tasty in comparison to the meat of the mule that had just died.

For a day they walked over a vast salt plain. The few brackish springs they found were thick with salt water. That night they located drinkable water; after drinking as much as they could tolerate, they pushed on through the night, hoping for better water ahead. Sometimes they spotted a pool of clear water in the distance. But when they rushed toward it, it disappeared—a mirage.

Through it all, Jed's two companions had not complained. Now Robert Evans staggered to a juniper tree and sank down.

"I've followed you . . . as far as I can . . . Jed," he panted. "This time I won't live to find out where we're going."

"We've got to push on and find water." Jed took him by the arm and helped him up. He pointed off in the distance. "See? There are mountains ahead. Come on, you can make it!"

"Those ain't no mountains out there," muttered Silas Gobel. "They're jest mirages, the kind we been seein' for days."

Trying his best to encourage the two men, Jed craned his neck and strained his eyes in search of water. The three men stumbled on.

Late one afternoon they dragged themselves toward a small cedar tree on the side of a sand hill. Here they dug holes and lay down in the cool sand. At the end of an hour they staggered on.

Shortly before sundown Jed squinted at several birds in the distance.

"Turtledoves!" he cried. "We can't be more than two or three miles from water!"

He spent an hour looking for a spring, but in the end he gave up. There was no water.

After a short rest they continued their march and traveled all night, with the imaginary sound of running water always in their ears. Later Jed would record in his journal: "In these moments how trifling were all those things that hold such an absolute sway over the busy and prosperous world. My dreams were not of gold or ambitious honors, but of my distant quite home, of murmuring brooks."

On the morning of June 25, it was the same old story: a journey over the desolate waste, a gleaming hot sun, a day more tormenting than the one before.

At ten o'clock Robert Evans' strength gave out and he collapsed under a scraggly cedar tree. "I can't go another step," he faltered. "Just go on without me and let me die."

Jed and Silas stared at each other. They were too exhausted to help him, or to argue. Even if they could lift him onto the back of the horse, it was too weak to carry him.

"We can't do any good by staying here to die with him," said Jed. "If we go on we might find water to save his life. There are snow-covered mountains in the distance—there's got to be water before that."

With sad hearts, Jed and Silas left Robert Evans behind. Forging ahead, they led the bony horse and mule. Jed's throat was too dry even to sing.

After they had gone a mile or two, they heard a gunshot from the direction they had come. Gunsmoke rose faintly over the spot where they had left Robert Evans.

Silas looked at Jed. "That's the end of Robert Evans," he said soberly, and Jed nodded.

They struggled on for another mile. Silas Gobel's head was bent and his feet dragged in the sand. Jed's throat was raw and parched, and without a word he threw himself on the baked sand.

"Dear Lord," he prayed, "if there's water here, please let us find it."

Then he got up and started to push forward. After a short distance he suddenly saw a flowing stream. *No,* he thought, *it's just another mirage.* He half-dragged himself several more yards. Then he looked again. The spring was still there.

"Water!" he shouted hoarsely. "Silas, there's a spring!"

Silas raised his head, looking around wildly. Then he saw the spring. Rushing toward it, he plunged his head into the fresh clear water and gulped. Jed knelt down and splashed water over his hot, sun-scorched face. The horse and mule, Jed and Silas, drank and drank until they could drink no more. Again Jed "lifted up his eyes unto the hills from whence came his help" as he thanked God for answered prayer. Surely they had "walked through the valley of the shadow of death," and the Lord had been with them.

Taking a kettle from the pack mule, Jed filled it with water. "I have to go back and see what happened to Robert. You stay here and rest, Silas."

"I hope you find him with his scalp on tight," Silas muttered gloomily.

Jed retraced his steps three miles to the little tree where they had left Evans. To Jed's surprise the man leaned his head on his elbow and looked up when Jed hurried toward him.

"Did you find . . . water?" Evans croaked.

"I have plenty," Jed said, handing him the kettle, which held four or five quarts.

Robert Evans grabbed it greedily and began to gulp. After he had emptied the kettle he handed it back to Jed.

"Why didn't you bring more?" he said, his eyes crinkling into a smile.

The water revived him enough to get him back on his feet. Yes, he had seen Indians, but when he had fired at them, they turned out to be mirages.

After Jed and Robert Evans reached Silas at the spring, the three men stayed there for the rest of the day, drinking a little water at a time and drying the spoiled horsemeat, their only food.

Indians appeared on the ridges and Jed made peace signs, but they rode away.

Early the next morning, refreshed and rested, the three men moved on. The springs along the way were salty, but finally Jed found one that was drinkable. Nearby was an Indian lodge with two braves, a squaw, and two children. At first the Indians seemed frightened.

Jed stepped forward and clasped his hands in the sign for friendship.

The Indians clasped their hands in answer and offered the three trappers some antelope meat. The three men ate and patted their stomachs in an exaggerated fashion to show the Indians their appreciation.

Their language was similar to that of the Snake Indians and Jed could understand some of it. They were Pahnakkees and said several days travel north would find buffalo.

Jed held both hands flat, nearly side by side with his palms up, with the right hand nearer his chest. Then he changed off, lifting them forward and drawing them back, to indicate tracks of feet walking.

"Where is the Salt Lake?" he asked. The Indians shrugged and shook their heads. Either they didn't know or couldn't understand.

That night Jed climbed a high ridge to the east, and in the far distance he saw what looked like a large body of water.

He hurried back to Robert and Silas. "I think I know now where we are!"

In the morning they trudged northward along another valley with many salt springs. Finally they rounded a ridge, and there, far to the north and east, lay the Great Salt Lake.

"No mirage could be that size ... could it?" said Robert Evans, finally letting go a laugh.

Forty-five miles to the east they came upon a river with banks almost overgrown with bulrushes and flags. Jed decided to cross it rather than go around it. He built a raft of cane grass by making sheaves and fastening them together. Then he piled on their camp equipment. Leading the horse, he swam the river; the mule followed. Then Jed turned about to help Robert and Silas, who paddled behind the raft.

Reaching the opposite shore, they built a fire, ate dried meat from the last horse that had died, and lay down to sleep.

The next morning they traveled fifteen more miles. Just before making camp Jed saw a bear.

Once, he took aim but had to break off to steady himself. The bear lumbered farther ahead. Again Jed took aim, this time getting off a shot. The bear faltered, then quickened its pace and disappeared from sight. Jed closed his eyes and sighed.

The next day Jed wounded a deer. As it staggered among the brush Jed stumbled after it, reloading as he went. Following the bloody tracks, he shot the deer again and dragged it back to camp, giddy with triumph.

Several days later, on Tuesday, July 3, 1827, about six weeks after they'd left the Stanislaus River, Jed Smith, Robert Evans, and Silas Gobel approached Bear Lake, ragged, hungry, exhausted. All that was left of the nine animals they had started out with from California was one skinny horse and one mule, both so weak they could hardly carry the few pitiful articles on their backs.

A lookout at the Bear Lake rendezvous (near present-day Laketown, Utah) had spotted the three haggard men while they were still some miles away and fired his rifle into the air. Now as the three men limped into camp, dozens of trappers and Indians ran shouting and cheering to meet them. A small cannon, brought to the rendezvous the year before by General Ashley, was fired in salute.

"Well, look at those scarecrows!" Billy Sublette said. "We'd given you up as lost."

"We thought we were lost too," Jed said with a tired sigh. "But God didn't let us down."

"Glad you didn't die tryin'," said Big Art Black, as he handed Jed a small pouch of berry pemmican.

They had crossed the Great Salt Lake desert and lived to tell about it. Among the Paiutes and Gosiutes of Skull Valley, Utah, oral tradition relates their first sight of white men in the valley: three ragged ones who came out of the shimmering Sandy Plain, to a spring where they plunged their heads into its waters. This crossing was something no white man had done before, something that would be remembered for years when men told stories about winning the West.

17
Keeping a Promise

For a few days Jedediah took time to answer letters from two of his brothers that had been waiting for him and write an account of his trip for the superintendent of Indian affairs, General William Clark himself. Then he was planning his trip back to California. True, he had already filled many white spaces on the map, but he had promised his men on the Stanislaus River he would return.

"And I'm going to keep my promise," he said.

"He's just itchin' to get back into the wilderness," Silas Gobel said with a wry smile.

"Why can't he forget about those men? They won't be there any more," said Robert Evans.

"Jed isn't like other men, don't forget. He said he'd be back. What he says he'll do, he does," said Silas.

"Then, you're going back with him?"

"Sure," Silas said stoutly. "I'd as soon follow him as anybody."

"Even after that . . . that inferno we just crossed?" Robert persisted.

"Maybe because of that."

"Huh?"

Silas scratched his balding gray head. "I dunno. Maybe I like the hymns, the way he sings 'em."

Although Jed had brought back no furs, his partners had caught enough to pay off the thirty-thousand-dollar debt to

Ashley. And they still had the large store of peltries Jed had left with the men in California.

Ten days after Jed's arrival, on July 13, the rendezvous ended and Jed was packed and ready to leave again.

Although Robert Evans decided not to go this time, eighteen other men agreed to join the party: They included Thomas Virgin, among the oldest and most seasoned of the trappers and after whom the Virgin River was named, Isaac Galbraith, a hunter and a giant of a man, Joseph La Point, and John Turner.

In his journal, Jed wrote that his main reason to return was to keep his promise to the trappers he had left on the Stanislaus, but he confessed the strange land lured him to explore the sea coast and all the land that lay between Mount St. Joseph and the sea.

Deciding he preferred the Mojave Desert to the Great Salt Lake Desert, Jed chose the longer, southern route back to California. Now familiar with the way ahead, he moved faster even though he led a larger group. They followed the Bear, Weber, and Provo rivers, then struck southwest to Utah Lake. Here Indians flocked toward him, telling him in signs and words he could understand that pale-faced people traveled through their country last summer and had left presents to prove their friendship. Jed was glad, for it meant less Indian trouble.

After trading gewgaws for food, they moved on. Jed rode southward along the Sevier River, picking up the trail of his earlier expedition, then adding shortcuts.

As they rounded the trail along the Santa Clara River, however, Jed came to an abrupt stop. Art almost rode into him. "What the—"

Silas Gobel edged up alongside him. "Last time we was through here, that was a village of farming Indians up ahead."

Art spit and wiped his mouth. "Maybe that was too much like white men's ways."

As the trappers picked their way through the burned-out

village they must have wondered how it had happened—accidently or deliberately.

Instead of traveling through the difficult Virgin River Canyon, Jed now detoured. They hiked up the Santa Clara about twenty-five miles, crossed the Beaver Mountains, and moved down Pautch Creek.

From Bitter Creek they went on to the mouth of the Virgin where they had crossed the Colorado River and made their way to the first Mojave village near the stream.

At first the Mojaves ran away. Later they came back with the sign of peace. Here Jed met Francisco, the Spanish-speaking half-breed who had been his interpreter earlier.

"Be careful," he warned Jed now. "White trappers kill many Mojave braves. They are in bad mood."

But they were so friendly Jed found it hard to believe. For three days Jed's party rested here, trading goods for beans, corn, dried pumpkins, and melons.

On August 18, Jed decided to move on across the river. Loading a few of their goods on rafts made of grass and reeds, he left ten men on shore to guard the horses and the rest of the supplies. With eight men he shoved out into the current.

Suddenly Art Black grabbed Jed's shoulder. "Look! Mojaves are attacking our men!"

Whirling around, Jed heard the shrill war whoops of Indians on the shore. Arrows struck his raft, wounding one man. Horrified, Jed saw Mojaves—with bow and arrow, war club and lance—falling upon his men on shore. Ten of them, among them Silas Gobel, were shortly killed. Paddling furiously, the men on the raft reached a sandbar. Jed knew their chances of staying alive were slim.

Streaming toward them were hundreds of Indians armed with arrows and clubs. All of Jed's horses were gone. Only nine men were left, and they were armed with just knives and five guns.

Tom Virgin stumbled toward the river, blood spurting from his head. Isaac Galbraith ran to him, dragged him into the river, and started to swim across. Arrows sang all around

109

them. As Tom and Isaac neared the shore, Jed and Art plunged into the water and pulled them ashore.

The Mojaves whooped and danced wildly. Having no time to wonder why the Indians had suddenly turned on them, Jed surveyed what they were left with: a small amount of powder, a few packs of gewgaws, and fifteen pounds of dried meat. Of the nine men, one was badly wounded.

Ahead lay a hundred fifty miles of inhospitable desert; behind them swarmed hundreds of blood-thirsty, yelling savages.

"Hurry!" Jed yelled. "Scatter the trinkets along the shore!" He was already ripping open one of the packs of gewgaws and pulling out handfuls of colored buttons, beads, and ribbons. "While they're fighting over these, we'll get away. Grab the packs and let's move. Quick!"

Everyone grabbed a pack while Art hoisted Tom Virgin on his back like a sack of meal and set out on a run. They had run less than a mile before the Mojaves had crossed the river and were fanning out to surround them.

"Back to the river!" Jed shouted, after a quick prayer for guidance. Plunging into the water, the men swam across toward a clump of cottonwoods.

Working madly, the trappers hacked down the brush with their knives and piled it high in front of them, forming a crude barricade. Joseph La Point fixed a bayonet to the end of his rifle.

Seeing this, Jed cried, "Cut down some of those saplings and tie your knives to the end of them. If we don't have time to get off any more shots, we'll use them."

"Are we going to make it, Jed?" asked Art Black.

When Jed saw the other men looking at him, he replied, "I think so." But in the privacy of his journal he admitted his doubts.

Four or five hundred Mojaves splashed through the water moving toward the pathetic little barricade on shore.

"Fire alternately!" Jed ordered. "Keep calm. And fire only when you're sure of hitting your mark. . . . Art, Isaac, Joseph—you fire first. While you're reloading, John and I will fire and then reload."

The men watched the Indians steal toward the river. Three braves stepped cautiously into the open.

"Fire!" Jed yelled. All three Indians staggered and fell.

The other warriors, seeing them fall, let out a howl of fright and fled. But would they come back?

Jed and his men waited, wondering when the Indians would return. Jed hoped the Mojaves preferred to do their fighting during the day like most other Indians he knew of. Finally, with the coming of darkness, he led his men off toward the desert. They plodded all night through shifting sands, Isaac Galbraith and Art Black taking turns carrying Tom Virgin. In the morning they found a spring.

"Drink all you can now, men," Jed ordered. "We have no way to carry water, and I don't know when we'll find another spring."

During the heat of the day the men stayed near springs, when they could be found, and traveled mostly at night when it was cooler. But in the dark it was also harder for Jed to spot familiar landmarks.

Although some of the men were nearly half-crazed with thirst, Jed tried to ignore his own parched throat. By now their dried meat was gone, so Jed cut up pieces of prickly pear cactus with his knife and told the men to start chewing.

"There's juice in them," he said, "and it will keep you going."

Day after day the weary men dragged themselves through the hot, blowing sand. Some dropped exhausted to the ground and Jed had to prod them to get back on their feet.

"Keep moving!" he urged. "The Lord won't let us die if we don't give up."

Walking, resting, walking, resting, the nine men pushed their way through the searing dust and burning sand until they reached a spring Jed had found the year before. From here he decided to turn west and head directly toward the salt plain he had crossed on his first venture over the Mojave Desert. They dug holes and covered themselves with cool sand and rested for the night. Still afoot, with little clothing to protect them from the burning sun, the men stumbled on the next morning until they reached the Mojave River. To Jed's dismay its bed was even drier than last year: No amount of digging produced any water.

After walking about eight miles upriver Jed spied two horses outside two Indian lodges. He must be careful not to frighten the Indians away.

Opening his packs, he showed his remaining gewgaws. The Indians' eyes lit up at the bolt of red cloth and blue beads in his outstretched hands.

"We need horses," Jed told them, using sign language. "We'll trade these bright goods for horses."

They nodded, eager for the trinkets. They even gave the men some cane grass candy and three stone jugs. Two horses among nine men were better than none, and Tom Virgin could ride now instead of being carried. If they got too hungry they could always kill the other horse.

Near the head of the river they came upon more Indians who pointed ahead at a blue blur against the western horizon. When Jed saw the gap in the San Bernardino Mountains ahead, he gave a shout—it was Cajon Pass.

"It won't be long now," he said. "We're near the end of our journey." Instead of following the course of the river as he had done on his first trip, Jed cut straight across the desert toward the pass. Making their way through a grove of Joshua trees (its sword-like leaves identifying it as a yucca plant) and into the canyon, the party pushed up the steep mountain trail.

When they reached the top, Jed stretched out his hand. "There it is, men. California!"

Driven by desperation and traveling night and day, Jed and his men had taken only nine and a half days to cross the desert from the scene of the massacre in the Mojave camp on the Colorado.

113

18

More Trouble with the Governor

Cattle belonging to the San Gabriel mission grazed quietly on the slopes, and the peaceful valley beckoned the hungry, thirsty men. That night they feasted on roast beef. Then they dried the rest of the meat to eat later, for Jed had allowed them to shoot a couple cows and to eat to their hearts' content.

He asked Isaac Galbraith and Tom Virgin to go to the mission and tell Father Sanchez about butchering the cattle.

"Tom, you stay at the mission until you're better," he said. "The people there are kind. When you've recovered you can join us in San Jose. Tell Father Sanchez to let the governor know we're here."

After resting awhile, Jed traded goods for more horses at a nearby settlement so he could join his men on the Stanislaus.

"I don't want to get into another fuss with Governor Echeandía," he told Art Black. "Father Sanchez will tell him I'm here. All I want is a permit to leave."

On Tuesday, September 18, 1827, only two days before the deadline Jed gave his trappers the spring before, he and the rest of the party rode north to meet the eleven men who had remained in California. When Jed reached their camp, a shout went up. There was hurrahing and backslapping and handshaking all around. But when Jed at last told them of the Mojave massacre, the loss of men and supplies, they

114

grew solemn, wondering about their own chances of getting back to Bear Lake alive.

Otherwise they were well, Harrison Rogers reported, and had had a good summer trapping. There was plenty of game and fresh berries for food. The Indians in the area had been friendly; even the patrol of Spanish soldiers that had encountered them had raised no objections to their presence.

Nevertheless, Jed decided this was no time to sit around, so he jumped briskly to his feet.

"Better pack up and get ready to move. Art Black and I will go to the Mission San Jose to get supplies for the trip."

"Which way are we heading?" asked Harrison Rogers. "It sure doesn't sound like a good idea to go back the way you came."

"That's for sure," said John Turner.

"And if you'd of seen 'em comin' into the rendezvous," Art Black added in his big voice, "you'd know gettin' over Mt. St. Joseph and crossing that Salt Lake Desert ain't no picnic neither!"

"We're heading north—to Oregon territory."

Jed had hoped to get out of California without crossing Governor Echeandía's path, but that was not to be. When he reached Mission San Jose, the friar, Narciso Duran, had heard of Jed's earlier trouble with the governor.

The priest looked straight at him. "I cannot give you supplies until you see the governor. He has not changed since you saw him last. But he does live in Monterey now, which should prove more convenient to you than a trip to San Diego ... which our people were having to make."

Jed's heart sank. He had thought to avoid the governor. This would surely delay leaving California, especially the rivalry for the governor's attention, implied by Father Duran. But Jed had no choice. The friars took his horses away and led him into the guardhouse. He tried to reason with them, but they refused to listen.

Jed chafed at being guarded. What could he do? He had heard of an American sailor named Welch who was on one of the ships and sent for him.

"He came immediately," Jed wrote in his journal, "but the reverend father refused to let me talk to him. I then tried to have an interview with the reverend father. He said that an officer would soon be down from San Francisco to ask about my business in the country. He asked if I had had anything to eat, perhaps thinking that I lived on faith instead of food!"

A few days passed before Lieutenant Ignacio Martinez of the Mexican army arrived. After a brief conversion the officer drew a deep breath.

"You will be placed on trial as an intruder and for claiming land along the Stanislaus River."

"Claiming land!" Jed was stunned. "On what grounds is the charge being made?" he asked finally, groping for words. "I haven't claimed any land."

"An Indian who was with you insisted you had said you had land here," the lieutenant barked.

"No, that is not true. He must have misunderstood," Jed protested. "Let me talk to him."

They brought the Indian before Jed, who cross-examined him. "Have you ever heard me make such a claim?" Jed asked.

The Indian confessed he had not. Other questions followed. At last, Jed was freed from the Indian's charge.

Father Duran frowned. "I hope you will leave now and stop your adventuring in our country."

"But I need supplies, horses, and a passport before I can leave," said Jed. "I can pay; we have furs."

"Furs! What do we want with furs? You are in too much of a hurry," the lieutenant growled. "We must first send a message to the governor."

Jed groaned. He certainly didn't want to see Governor Echeandía. But there was nothing to do except wait. Day after day Jed and Art chafed while waiting word from the governor.

After two weeks had dragged by, the long-awaited letter came, together with a guard to escort Jed to the Governor's mansion in Monterey. When Art started to accompany Jed, the officer in charge gave an order and three soldiers pointed their rifles at Art.

"El hombre grande no va!" barked the officer, shaking his head.

Jed grinned. "I guess you're too big to go, Art."

Art continued to stare at the soldiers who held their rifles on him, but his arms relaxed and the big hands unclenched.

The journey took three days.

When they reached Monterey at eleven o'clock that night, Jed was thrown into the *calabozo* and guarded closely. He tossed restlessly all night.

At eleven the next morning the governor sent for him.

"So! You're here again," Echeandía greeted him coldly. He was furious that the "wild *yanqui*" had popped up again to give him trouble, and he was sick of the whole mess. If he kept Jed in jail, the American government might get angry; then the Mexican government would heap all the blame on the governor. If on the other hand, he let Jed roam freely in California, the governor's enemies would accuse him of giving foreigners free rein.

"Captain Smith," he said, "what you have told me about your business may be true, but I cannot believe it. When you came to San Diego last year you said you had traveled to California along a dry, barren desert. Now you have come that way again."

"Your Excellency," Jed said politely, "it's true that when I was at San Diego I said the route was very bad. But my route back was much worse; it couldn't be used for horses loaded with pelts. So I thought it best to come by the first route."

"So, as you say, you came to get your party on the Stanislaus River. But why did you not do me the courtesy of notifying me as soon as you entered my country?"

"When I came I sent word immediately to Father Sanchez. I assumed the good padre would forward word of my presence to you. . . . All I want is horses so I can take my men out of California."

The governor wasn't quite satisfied with the explanation.

117

"Come back in three days and I will decide what to do with you," he said. "But don't expect me to be easy on a man who acts like a spy!"

Spy. Here was that hateful word again!

The governor hoped the British and American merchants in the city would sign a paper promising Jed would behave and leave. Then if anything happened, he could blame the merchants. Jed hurried to his friend Captain Cooper and other sailors for help. Finally, on November 12, 1827, the governor gave Jed a choice of three things: wait until orders came from Mexico, go to Mexico himself, or leave California by the way he had come.

Jed chose to leave California.

After days of hassling, Jed received his papers. After finding buyers of his peltries among the merchantmen, he boarded the *Franklin* with close to four thousand dollars and sailed up the coast for the straggling village of San Francisco to meet his trappers. He had agreed to sell the peltries for four thousand dollars to pay for supplies. The next two weeks he was busy buying supplies at San Jose. They would travel east for some miles, then head north.

Jed found his men baling furs and goods for the northward trek when he arrived back at the camp on the Stanislaus. He put two blacksmiths to work repairing guns. But Isaac Galbraith, a free trapper, asked to stay in California.

"I believe Governor Echeandía is going to grant me license to stay, Captain; I think hunting here can make me a good living. Sorry to disappoint you," said the big man.

Reluctantly Jed accepted his resignation and consoled himself with the fact that he was also picking up some good men, among them Richard Leland, a little Englishman big on adventure.

December 8 was observed as a holy day at the Mission San Jose, so their party could do little work. The next day was Sunday and Jed went to Mass with Father Duran. He enjoyed the music of violins, bass violas, and flutes.

Several days later Tom Virgin, who had been detained in San Diego by authorities, rode into camp. Jed gave the old man a warm welcome. Tom told him that the Indian who got them into trouble had been sentenced to be shot.

"But that's not fair!" Jed protested. "He doesn't deserve to die."

"Easy, son," he told Jed. "The rest of the story is that Father Sanchez obtained his pardon."

"Good. I would've felt very sorry if I had been to blame for his death."

Again Father Sanchez had shown his Christian character, asking the authorities for mercy on behalf of another.

Governor Echeandía had set a date for Jed to leave and time was running out. The last peltries were baled and supplies bagged and boxed. All Jed needed was a way to ferry across the river with his goods. After a frantic search and many delays, the needed boat turned up.

Now as they were ready to ferry their goods to the other side, there was no sign of James Reed and Louis Pombert.

"Reed didn't forget your chastising him for his lack of manners with the padres, Jed," said Harrison Rogers.

"It appears that the man still lacks the common courtesies. If he doesn't show up, he can explain himself to Echeandía. I hope he's learned some Spanish. We'll not be staying around for another audience!"

Looking for the two missing trappers wasn't easy. The stream was high with rain, so Jed sent Indian scouts to search. They returned, saying they had found tracks but no men. Two trappers went down one side of the river while Jed and another trapper scoured the other side. Yet the missing men couldn't be found. Other Indian scouts joined the hunt. Reed and Pombert had vanished.

When Jed discovered that the two trappers had taken with them all their belongings—plus eleven of Jed's forty-eight traps—it dawned on him that they would not see them again.

19

Up the Wild Coast

Finally having a stock of supplies, Jed led his party north through the miry swamps of the Sacramento River valley. His men driving 350 horses and mules had their hands full, so they decided to spend the rest of the winter in the valley.

"Having been so long absent from the business of trapping and so much perplexed and harassed by the folly of men in power," wrote Jed in his journal, "I returned again to the woods, the river, the prairie, the camp and the game with a feeling somewhat like that of a prisoner escaped from his dungeon and chains."

When the weather warmed, they crossed the Sacramento River and worked their way toward a pass Jed thought he could see in the distant Sierra Nevada Mountains.

Now and then Indians whooped from the hills, but as Jed approached with the peace sign they fled. Although the men found a steady supply of beaver, their catch was limited by the loss of traps to Reed and Pombert.

Now a new menace faced them. The Sierra foothills swarmed with bears. A grizzly seemed to crouch behind every bush, and it wasn't unusual to see fifty or sixty bears a day.

On Saturday, March 8, Harrison Rogers and John Hanna shot one bear and wounded another, which fled. The two men decided to follow it and finish it off. When they came upon it, however, the bear had other ideas.

Hanna rushed into camp, shouting, "The little booshway's

been attacked!" Jed grabbed his possibles bag with his medical supplies and the two raced back to the thicket where Rogers lay, with blood gushing from a dozen deep gashes. Jed washed the wounds and treated them with a salve of soap and sugar, then got him back to camp.

For two weeks Jed held the men in camp until Rogers could ride again, remembering his own agony after he had tangled with a bear. "But at least you won't have to grow your hair long to cover a mangled ear," Jed told him.

One day after Jed himself shot a grizzly, he was walking toward it when Art boomed out, "He's alive!"

But from where Jed was, he could see no movement. Indeed, the bear he shot was dead—but a second bear sprang up from behind it, and with a roar charged. Without hesitation, Jed dropped his empty gun and dived into the creek, saying later, "I guess a grizzly with its mouth open makes me nervous."

The grizzly, continuing its charge, bowled Art aside as if he were a child and went for Joseph La Point, whose rifle was also empty.

La Point, however, had his bayonet fixed to his rifle. He jumped out of the bear's path, thrusting and withdrawing his rifle as he did so. The bear skidded to a halt, seemingly puzzled by the sudden pain in its side. It then lunged at La Point. But the man parried one of the bear's paws and ran the bayonet into the animal's neck. Rising high on its hind legs, the bear roared. For a moment the bear hung there above the man—who gently, like a cobra, waved before the animal's face a bloody bayonet. Suddenly the animal dropped to all fours and padded off.

Brushing himself off, Art walked over to La Point. "I think I'm going to get me one of those things," he said, pointing to the bayonet on the end of La Point's rifle.

Later the same day, as Jed rode through the trees, another bear charged him. His frightened horse bolted, but Jed was able to control the animal and galloped away. Even so, the bear grabbed the horse's tail and hung on for forty or fifty yards before giving up. He noted in his journal that he had been "quite glad to get rid of his company."

One day Jed met a tribe of friendly Indians. They seated him on a mat as they visited.

"If missionaries want a place to work," he told Harrison Rogers later, "they should come to this valley. These Indians are honest and peace-loving."

Harrison Rogers agreed.

On April 11 they camped on the west bank of the Sacramento for two days while hunting beaver, and in a single night they caught twenty with only twenty-eight traps.

As the party started north again, Jed's eyes searched for a trail through the mountains. Fog rolling in from the sea like an earthbound cloud often hid the way ahead and it became impossible to see the gaps in the mountain range. Jed chafed under the constant fog and rain.

The trappers ran into snags, fallen trees, and giant slippery rocks. Travel became difficult and often treacherous. Some of the men shoved ahead to cut a path with axes, while the rest tried to ride herd on the frightened horses and mules. Sharp branches clutched at the men's shirts and tore them to shreds. Sometimes they made only two or three miles in ten hours. Looking like watery sunlight, mists dampened the tired trappers and made them even more uncomfortable.

"Well, at least the trapping's been good," groused Art.

Discouraged in his search for a pass through the Sierra Nevada Mountains, Jed finally turned back toward the coast.

Even then, the party often had to force its way along the sides of steep, stony hills, through heavy thickets, and among rough masses of rock. The pack animals developed sore feet from the stony trail. Two were crowded off the path by the other animals and fell into the river below, carrying with them some traps, supplies, and personal possessions of some of the men.

To make matters worse, unfriendly Indians stalked their footsteps almost daily.

Jed marched up and down his line of men and animals

as they plodded along. "Keep moving!" he barked. "Don't let the Indians pick you off with their arrows!"

Although giant firs and pines provided shade and there was plenty of water, it was one of the roughest journeys Jed had made.

For more than two months the party pushed slowly down the Klamath River before traveling with any degree of ease toward the Oregon coast. Besides the huge sand dunes, the coastal stretch featured lush forests and fresh-water lakes and streams. Colossal rock formations rose from the sea and wild flowers dotted the dunes.

The coastal Indians, who ate fish and lived in log lodges, puzzled Jed. Sometimes they were friendly, eager to trade otter skins, fish, and berries for gewgaws. At other times they shot his horses with arrows. Now and then some followed his camps and seemed glad to see him; others fled when he came near.

(From an old Indian account of a meeting with Jed, who led a "strange animal," it seems that the horse may have been quite unknown and therefore feared by Indians of this area.) "We can't trust these Indians," Jed told Harrison and Art.

"At least not all of them," said Harrison.

"Maybe not any of them," said Jed, eyeing a couple of braves through the trees. "Remember what I said about the way the Mojaves behaved . . . right up to the last."

"Right up to the last," echoed Art, nodding his shaggy head. "You need eyes in the back of your head around here."

The first sign of real danger came when, after the men camped in a deep ravine, Jed discovered an arrow sticking in the neck of a horse.

"Get your guns!" he ordered.

Suddenly a dozen Indians were shooting into their camp. The trappers chased them, wounding three. After yelling around the camp until nightfall, the Indians left. As the party moved west, Indians followed along the ridges all day long. Again and again Jed and several trappers went toward them and showed them by signs that they wanted to be friends.

"Friends!" Art Black snorted. "Might as well make friends with a rattlesnake."

Winding up steep, rough trails, Jed spotted more trouble as Indians sniped at their horses. Jed and Art approached them with a peace sign, but the Indians pranced in circles, getting ready to train their bows on them.

"Maybe if we shoot at them we'll scare them off," Jed suggested.

"Nothing would pleasure me more," Art said, taking aim.

The Indians scurried away, shooting arrows as they fled. But they pestered Art and Jed until the two men got on their horses and gave chase. This time they wounded two Indians, which badly frightened the rest. After that the Indians didn't come back.

As company clerk, Harrison Rogers had made a gloomy entry in his logbook:

"Two men were wounded today. That makes six men hurt in five days. Two men are too weak to walk. . . . We've lost twenty-seven mules in five days."

One night Jed laid aside his Bible and read the entry, shaking his head. Then he began to pace back and forth from one end of the camp to the other. Art Black watched him from his blanket.

"Wonder when in thunder that man sleeps," he muttered. "He's always moving up and down, it seems. Always looking for a better trail or scoutin' for Indians."

"Go back to sleep, Art," John Hanna growled. "Quit worryin' about him. He ain't human, that's what."

Rain fell in a slow, steady drizzle that soaked the spongy ground and made walking a labor. The party was forced to camp often and let the tired, lame horses rest.

Harrison Rogers, still weak from his grizzly wounds and feeling the effects of their toilsome progress, made another entry in his journal: "Oh, God, may it please Thee in Thy divine providence to still guide and protect us through this wilderness of doubt and fear, as Thou hast done to now, and be with us in the hour of danger and difficulty; as all praise is due to Thee and not to man."

Jed had hoped that once they reached the Pacific Ocean they would move north to the Columbia River. But the beach was either very rocky or consisted of outright cliffs, delaying their progress. Always there was fog and spitting rain or mist and the men's bodies ached from the damp weather. With very little game to shoot in the desolate country, they were often hungry. Now and then friendly Indians offered them seaweed and whale blubber and a few shellfish.

On a Monday afternoon in early June, Jed rode through the territory looking for food. As his horse stumbled along he began to pray.

"Dear Lord, You have helped us in the past, and You know my men are suffering. Won't You please be merciful and help us now?"

Riding around the bend he saw a small herd of elk and shot three. Elated, he rode back into camp. The Lord had answered prayers again, as He had done so often before.

"Men!" he shouted, "I need a couple of men and pack horses."

"What for, Captain?"

"You'll see soon enough." And he smiled a bit.

When they got to the vicinity of the kill, Jed pointed toward the elk he had shot. The men let out a whoop and, pulling out their knives, raced toward the elk.

Pushing on and losing more horses along the way, the party reached the Pacific Ocean on June 13 (just south of present day Crescent City). Traveling was a bit easier close to the beach.

Ten days later, Jed's party reached what is now the Oregon-California border. It was a day that Harrison Rogers in his journal pronounced "good."

20

Massacre

As Jed's party worked its way up the Oregon coast, hostile Indians still shot at their horses. Here the coast was rough, with rock-strewn beaches and high ridges. Sometimes the animals slid from precipices. Near the end of June, twelve drowned while swimming across the turbulent Rogue River.

Once, they met two friendly Indians who spoke the Chinook Jargon. To go up from the Rogue River, the Indians said, would bring them to another "water."

"Wel Hamett—Wel Hamett," they said, gesturing north.

Jed nodded. "Yes? You say we are near the Willamette River? That is good." It was what he'd hoped for—to reach the Willamette River before long.

At Coos Bay, nearly a hundred Coos Indians visited the party, bringing mussels, fish, and berries to trade. Jed bought a fine sea otter pelt from the chief.

Jed noticed that the Coos seemed more civilized, having cloth, knives, and blankets. In a friendly gesture, Jed asked to examine some of the goods more closely and showed them to Richard Leland.

"Aye, British. We're in Hudson's Bay Company territory now for sure, Cap."

It bothered him a little, knowing they might run into rival trappers.

The Indians seemed friendly and wanted to trade. They brought beaver pelts and elk meat and appeared well sat-

126

isfied with what they got in exchange. But Jed was cautious, always on the lookout for trouble.

"Take care how you treat an Indian," he warned his men again. "Our lives may depend upon your actions toward them."

Now they reached the Umpqua River, a gray-brown muddy stream that reminded Jed of the Missouri. Here they planned to camp for several days before pushing on.

But things went wrong from the first day. After the Indians had traded, one brave eyed one of the trapper's horses sharply, as though planning to steal the animal.

"Get away!" the trapper shouted angrily. "Scat! Git—now!" Harrison Rogers tried to smooth matters out, but the Indian whirled around and stalked sullenly away.

On Saturday, fifty Kelawatset Indians camped nearby for the night. That spelled trouble, for Jed had heard of their untrustworthiness. Indeed, an Indian did steal the only axe the trappers had. To recover it, Jed had him tied up until he promised to return it. The Indian did so, but he was a chief and such treatment did not go down very well. So for a time the trappers stood with their guns cocked and ready. But the Indians backed off. Instead, they brought furs to trade the next day.

Sunday morning Jed called to Richard Leland and John Turner. "I don't want to wear out our welcome here. Tomorrow we'll see if we can't get a guide and canoe up one of these streams and look for a trail north to the Willamette."

As Monday, July 14, 1828, dawned, Jed grew uneasy, for he noticed the Indians were gathering in rather large numbers around the camp. He ordered Harrison Rogers to keep an eye on the Indians.

"Don't let any Indians into camp while we're gone," he warned Rogers. "Oil your guns and pack up. We'll leave as soon as we know where the best trail is." Then Jed and his two men left.

With their Indian guide they traveled up a small stream

by canoe. They had gone a short way when Jed sat up straight.

"Here's a good crossing for our supplies!" he shouted. He began to turn the canoe around and start back for camp. Suddenly an Indian appeared on the bank and called to the guide. Before Jed realized what had happened, the guide had grabbed Jed's rifle and dived into the river. At that moment Jed heard the sound of distant gunfire—the camp! Suddenly other Indians appeared along the bank and began firing at the men in the canoe.

Jed and the two men bent their backs to the paddle and sent the canoe cutting across the water to the opposite shore.

"Dive under water and make for the other side!" he yelled to his two companions. After the shooting stopped, Jed, Richard, and John sputtered to the surface. Their guide was climbing out on the opposite bank, brandishing his prize of Jed's rifle.

The three men ran into the woods and waited until the Indians on the bank stopped shooting at them and faded back into the woods. Quietly the three trappers made their way toward the camp. Jed climbed a hill and looked at the scene below. His heart almost stood still at the gruesome sight.

Jed turned and looked away. Finally he said, "There's no movement down there. They've killed them all ... taken everything. Nothing left to do but save our own skins. We'd better get out of here while we're in one piece."

With a heavy heart Jed turned away from a scene he would never forget, men he would never forget: Harrison Rogers, old Tom Virgin, Joseph La Point, Art Black ...

For days the three pushed their way through brush and rocky beaches, living on roots and berries. Sorrowfully Jed moved ahead of his two men, his back bent and his scarred, hawk-like face thrust forward. His blue bandanna streamed like a sail behind him.

In a few days the three men reached a Tillamook Indian village where they were treated kindly. After resting and eating, they plodded on, making out on roots and berries;

Fort Vancouver, the Hudson's Bay Company's trading post on the Columbia River, was now their only hope for safety.

On August 10, a Sunday, Captain Jedediah Smith, Richard Leland, and John Turner stumbled up to the gate of the trading post. The three half-starved, barefooted, ragged men staggered in more dead than alive. Jed was almost bowled over when a familiar face greeted them:

"Jed!"

"Art! Art Black!" Jed cried. "What are you doing here? You escaped!"

The big man, his eyes downcast, could only nod. "It's a sorry story, Jed."

That night after the men were fed and settled into comfortable chairs, Arthur Black told what had happened.

21

White-headed Eagle

Three days before the arrival of Jed and his two men, Art had been brought in by friendly Indians. He had been so weak he could hardly stand.

At first he could not even make sense. When he did regain his composure he told them he was the sole survivor of an American fur company that Jedediah Smith had led northwest from California. Now Art continued with his story.

"After you left camp," said Art, "some of us were eatin' by the fire, some of us were cleanin' rifles—like you said to do—and some of the others were fastenin' canoes together so's we could carry our goods across the river when you came back." He looked at the floor for a time. "Then a scuffle seemed to break out, and then there was a shout—by one of the Indians—a signal, I reckon . . ."

Art paused again, and cleared his throat.

Then out had come hidden knives and clubs, as more than a hundred Indians rushed them. The trappers had grabbed their rifles and jumped to their feet, but a battery of clutching arms and strangle-holds had thrown them to the ground. With a fierce yell, the Kelawatsets fell upon their victims, then pranced on the bloody ground, pouncing on the white men's packs.

"I was on the outskirts of the camp when I heard the yells. Two Indians jumped me, wantin' my rifle. A third one was coming from behind with a hatchet. I jumped to one side but he caught me on the back of my shoulder. So I let go my rifle and hightailed it for the woods."

Sure that the Indians would be after him if he headed for the Willamette, he turned toward the coast. After two weeks of aimless wandering with only berries for food, and more than one brush with more Indians, he finally stumbled into an encampment of Indians.

"By then I was done in," he said, "and decided to turn myself over to them, hoping they'd be kind. I figured bein' killed by them couldn't of been any worse than starvin' to death or being ate by grizzlies."

But the Indians were Tillamook and friends of the Hudson's Bay Company. They fed him and brought him to Fort Vancouver. There he had been received by Dr. John McLoughlin, agent for the Hudson's Bay Company.

Six feet four inches tall, with a full head of white hair, McLoughlin was an imposing figure. The Indians called him the White-headed Eagle. But despite his fierce look and all his authority in the region, he was known for his fairness and firmness with the Indians. A Canadian, born of an Irish father and Scotch mother on October 19, 1784, he had studied medicine in Scotland; among the Indians who flocked to the fort with their ills he had become known as Old Man Doctor.

Although Fort Vancouver (located across the river from what is now Portland, Oregon) was remote and secluded, it was an island of civilization in the wilderness. Many of McLoughlin's officers were well-educated, being graduates of the best universities in Britain. In their spare time they read history, biography, books on travel and agriculture, poetry, and the London *Times;* the fort housed its own library. Worship on Sunday was as much a part of life at the post as trade with the Indians. And, unlike the American practice, families were a part of the British approach to the fur trade.

Dr. McLoughlin paid the Indians for their kindness of bringing in the big white man. Thinking Smith and his two companions might have escaped too, since they were not in the camp when the Indians attacked, the good doctor had sent Indian runners to the Willamette chiefs with gifts of tobacco, asking them to scour the valley for the missing men.

"Whoever hurts the white men," McLoughlin had warned, "will be punished. But whoever brings them safely to the fort will be rewarded." Yet so far no one had been found.

Thus on August 10, as the fort's party was planning to leave on a search for the three men, Smith, Turner, and Leland had stumbled into the fort.

Jed was chagrined by Art Black's story. Against orders, his men had allowed the Kelawatsets into camp. Before the men had put their guns back together, the Indians had attacked.

"Sometimes you escape, sometimes you don't, I guess," said Art. "I thought I'd seen the last of you, since you left with an Indian guide. I'm glad he got just your rifle and not your scalp."

After the men had rested and the doctor had looked after their physical needs, he called Jed to his office.

"I realize that our countries have an agreement of joint occupancy of the Oregon Territory. But you Americans seem to have a knack for causing trouble. In your trapping of this territory, you have angered the Indians. So far they have not bothered us. But you have made things difficult, you know." McLoughlin paced about slowly. With a cane he favored his left leg.

Jed nodded. "That's something I can't deny, I'm sorry to say." Jed thought, *I wanted to explore the West, fill the empty places on the maps, and earn money to help my family. But now I've lost it all—including my maps and journals.*

McLoughlin stopped pacing, at the same time interrupting Jed's musing. "However, I've heard good things about you, Captain Smith. You're a Christian gentleman who hasn't lost his faith in this wilderness, which many describe as being God-forsaken. I don't accept that . . . and you're reason enough not to."

133

Jed blinked. "I apologize, sir—what did you say I hadn't lost?"

"Your faith, son, you haven't lost your faith."

A smile began to light Jed's face. "You're right, sir. That's true. I haven't lost my faith. . . . Thank you for reminding me."

McLoughlin continued. "The truth of the matter is, Captain Smith, when your Mr. Black arrived here, I was ready to dispatch a party of my men to see what they could see." Here he paused. "But now let us talk to Alex McLeod. He's the head of my trappers and he knows this country. I'll send him and some of my men to recover your stolen goods, if possible."

"That's more than I deserve, sir."

"Then let us call it the Lord's mercies, which we all enjoy without deserving." He rubbed his brow. "At the same time it will be a lesson to the Indians. They are sometimes wayward children and must be shown correction."

Calling the tall, slim Alex McLeod from the nearby cabin, McLoughlin told him of his plans.

"An American trapper has been robbed, and most of his men killed. Take forty men and go to the Umpqua River and recover everything you can."

Jed rose to his feet. "I would like to accompany your party, sir."

"Captain Smith," said McLoughlin, clearing his throat, "as a doctor, I am bound to remind you of your condition due to exposure and deprivation. You need your rest."

"Perhaps. But more than that, I need to see if any more of my men survived. And those that didn't," Jed drew in a deep breath and it came out a sigh, "they stand in need of a decent burial."

The doctor's face softened and he nodded. "I understand, son."

On Saturday, September 6, McLeod, Jed, and several Canadian trappers left Fort Vancouver in a boat up the Willamette River. The rest traveled overland under Lieutenant

Thomas McKay. With McKay were Art Black, John Turner, and Richard Leland.

When the party reached the Umpqua River several days later, Indians along the river fled, but soon returned.

The next day Starnoose, an Umpqua chief, came to camp with eight of Jed's horses. Starnoose, friendly toward the white men, had visited the Kelawatsets, who had traded for their loot.

"Will Hudson's Bay chief make war on the Kelawatsets?" Starnoose asked.

"No. We want to recover Captain Smith's property. That is all."

"Then we will help you," Starnoose said, for the Umpquas feared the powerful British as well as the Kelawatsets.

Together with the Umpqua chief, the McLeod party swept down the Umpqua River. Indians from each village along the waterway surrendered loot they had received in trade from the Kelawatsets: beaver and otter skins, horses, rifles, pistols, traps, kettles, beads, clothing, books, maps, and bottles of medicine.

Near the mouth of the river the expedition came upon the scene of the massacre at Jed's camp. Eleven skeletons lay bleaching in the sun. Four were missing, perhaps taken captive and tortured.

As McLeod and his men dug graves and buried the eleven skeletons in the rain and fog, Jed thought of the men who had been with him since 1826: "Little Booshway" Harrison Rogers, Abraham LaPlant, John Hanna, Tom Virgin and others—some of the eight who had cheated death at the hands of the Mojaves. He thought of Art Black's words, *"Sometimes you get away, sometimes you don't."*

And then he thought of Paul's words to the Romans, reciting them aloud:

"Whether we live, we live unto the Lord; and whether we die, we die unto the Lord: whether we live therefore, or die, we are the Lord's. For to this end Christ both died, and rose, and revived, that he might be Lord both of the dead and the living."

Finally he prayed, commending the fallen men to the Lord "who knows the hearts of all men."

North from the mouth of the Umpqua and along the coast to Siuslaw River the expedition marched on, gathering skins, goods, and horses. Near Ten-Mile Creek they found Indians who had bartered for Harrison Rogers' and Jed's precious journals.

For the first time in days Jed's face brightened at the dirty, water-stained belongings. "Now I have my journals and maps again!"

The party returned to Fort Vancouver in early December in a downpour of rain, their trip hampered by swollen rivers.

When Jedediah Smith stomped into the fort, shaking off his waterlogged moccasins, he was given news that made him groan. He was about to meet with the governor general of the Hudson's Bay Company, Sir George Simpson. *Oh, Lord, what does this governor want?*

22

Wintering at Ft. Vancouver

While Jed and McLeod were still on the Umpqua, Sir George Simpson had come to Fort Vancouver on an official visit. As governor general of the Hudson's Bay Company, he was on a tour of the western posts.

After the search party returned to the fort, the governor had a long chat with Jed. A pudgy but energetic man, he was only four years older than Jed.

"It has cost us several thousand dollars to recover your property," Governor Simpson told Jed. He had listened to the story of the massacre on the Umpqua River and knew of the efforts of Hudson's Bay men to help Jed recover his goods.

Jed turned away uncomfortably. He had appreciated their help but he regretted the cost to the rival company.

"If only I could repay you," Jed said darkly.

"We don't want you to repay us," Sir George went on quickly, seeing Jed's discomfort.

"You are very kind," Jed managed in a tight voice. "If there's anything I can do, anything to help—"

"There is." He put his hands together at the fingertips. "For one thing, you can let me take your recovered furs off your hands." Before Jed could offer a protest, Sir George added immediately, "At a fair price, sir!" Then, shaking his head, he continued, "Really, Captain Smith, your peltries are in a terrible shape. In the first place, they've been poorly dressed and exposed to rain for months."

Jed nodded. "I guess you're right. What do you suggest?"

"I'll pay three dollars each for the beaver, two dollars for the land otter, and ten dollars for the sea otter. For the horses I'll pay ten dollars apiece."

Altogether Sir George offered Jed about $2,600 for the furs and horses recovered along the Umpqua.

Drawing a deep breath, Jed said, "Of course, if my men and I could ship our furs to the Walla Walla River ourselves and get them to Pierre's Hole for the rendezvous—"

"That would be foolish," Sir George cut in. "You don't know the country. Our trappers are familiar with the Indians in this area and we never send less than thirty or forty men to guard our shipments. Also, making your way over snow-covered mountains means traveling on snowshoes. Have you ever done that?"

Jed smiled slowly. "There are many things I had never done . . . until I did them."

"Yes, well, that may be. . . . But think of this, my good man: Recovering your property has cost us around five thousand dollars. Now," he held up his hands as if to counter any further apology by Jed, "I'll charge that up to kindness to a fellow white man. But you should consider my offer of taking your horses and furs off your hands—even though you think you *might* do better."

Jed had to admit to himself that Sir George knew what he was talking about. It would be much harder for Jed to get his furs to the rendezvous over unknown territory; he had already experienced that.

"When spring comes, we'll take you with us to the Red River," continued the governor. "From there you'll make your way easily by canoe down the Missouri. Meanwhile, we want you to stay here at the fort as our guests. You know winter is no time to travel."

Agreeing with this governor was not nearly as hard as it had been to agree with the governor in California. Jed found this stout, talkative man likable. Furthermore, Jed thought to himself, the hospitality extended to him and his men was

138

much more agreeable than that offered by the authorities in California.

Jed relaxed during the winter months, enjoying the kindness of Dr. McLoughlin and Sir George. An added pleasure was the Sunday services and morning prayers that were part of life at the fort. Officers and educated men thanked God before they ate meals of roast beef, boiled mutton, baked salmon, beets, carrots, turnips, potatoes, and wheat bread.

During the cold snowy days when the fort was snug and warm, Jed told about his trips to California. The Hudson's Bay Company plainly saw that "shrewd, intelligent" Mr. Smith had discovered a rich untapped beaver country farther south.

As Jed shared his reports, he drew maps for his rivals in the fur trapping trade. They also discussed problems with the two groups trapping in the same territory.

Jed thought, *Why can't we each have our own trapping territory? What if my men and I trap on the east side of the Great Divide and let the British trap on the west side?*

"I'll agree to stay out of your trapping lands," Jed said finally. He really owed the Hudson's Bay Company something for the trouble he had caused them, and for their help.

"What did I tell you, Sir George?" boomed Dr. McLoughlin. "This Captain Smith is a Christian we can trust. He gives us valuable information, and lets us have the territory to ourselves besides."

On Wednesday, March 11, 1829, after the spring thaws sent ice crashing down the rivers, Jedediah Smith packed his belongings, ready to strike out for Pierre's Hole, where he had agreed to meet Billy Sublette, Davey Jackson, and their trappers.

Although Richard Leland had other plans and John Turner had been offered a job as a guide, Art Black decided to stick with Jed.

"A winter here's enough for me," said Art.

The two men paddled upriver on the Columbia, trapping along the way and pushing toward the place of the rendezvous. Their route would take them beyond the site of the present Grand Coulee Dam, to the Hudson's Bay posts of Fort Colville and Kettle Falls, near the northeastern corner of what would become the state of Washington, down into Montana to the present city of Missoula, up the Bitter Root Valley, and across the divide to the Salmon River.

Rumors had drifted to Billy Sublette that Hudson's Bay Company had done away with Jed and his trappers and had seized their peltries, but Davey Jackson didn't believe this.

"It's time to look for Jed; it's been almost two years," said Davey.

"I thought you didn't care for meeting any Hudson's Bay 'representatives'!" said Billy.

"I ain't going to meet nobody—I'm going to get Jed."

About mid-July, as Jed and Art made their way along the trail in what is now northwestern Montana, Jed saw several figures plodding on the trail ahead and jerked Art behind a tree.

"Indians?" asked Art.

Jed peered around the tree. "No ... I don't think so. As a matter of fact, that looks like Davey Jackson."

Sure enough, one of his partners was leading a horse packed with a few beaver, some sea otter skins, and the hide of a moose.

After a hearty handshake when they met, Davey drew a sharp breath. "Well, you don't look too much the worse for wear. But what's been keepin' you?"

"The White-headed Eagle himself," declared Jed.

"Huh?"

So Jed began to catch his partner up on what had happened to him and his men over the last two years.

When the party reached the rendezvous at Pierre's Hole, at the western base of the Teton Mountains, Jed's news for his other partner wasn't good: twenty-four of their men massacred, great losses of supplies and furs, horses, and traps. But he had with him the money the Hudson's Bay Company had paid him, plus a part of the four thousand dollars he had received for furs sold in San Francisco.

Jed had good news too. "I discovered that the Hudson's

Bay Company's dealings are fair and just, and their furs are much better than ours. I've learned some good things from them."

While the rough trappers enjoyed their usual brawling good time, the partners discussed their problems. They had suffered three bad years, and the future seemed uncertain. Jed said that southwest of the Great Salt Lake was not beaver country, California meant trouble with the Spanish, and the Snake River country was almost trapped out with both the British and Americans working it. To the north the land was still rich in beaver—if they wanted to fight the Blackfeet Indians.

After spending the rest of the summer in Pierre's Hole, Jed insisted on carrying out the vow he had made at the Hudson's Bay Company, that the Americans would stay away from the area of the Hudson's Bay Company and not compete with them.

"We'll leave the Snake River country to the British," he said. "I owe them that much."

23

Thoughts of Home

In their planning and talking, the three partners hit upon an unheard-of scheme. Billy Sublette would go to St. Louis to buy merchandise to sell at the next rendezvous to be held at Wind River—and carry it overland across the mountains in wagons instead of by keelboat up the Missouri.

The idea was exciting. No one had ever tried this before, although freight wagons traveled regularly along the Santa Fe Trail across the Midwest prairies to the Southwest. It would be a new venture for shipping furs to St. Louis, and it might work.

As he had done on a similar mission three years earlier, Billy Sublette chose Moses Black Harris to go with him. They would travel the fifteen hundred miles to St. Louis in the dead of winter. Jed took the opportunity to send several letters along for his worried family.

To his brother Ralph he wrote:

> God has made me a steward of a small pittance, and my prayer is that while I am allowed the privilege of using it I may use it without abusing it. If any of our friends are in distress, please let me know. Let it be my greatest pleasure that we can enjoy the height of our ambition now, when our parents are in the decline of life, to smooth the pillow of their age, and as much as is in us lives, take from them all cause of trouble. It is that I may be able to help those who stand in need

that I face every danger. It is for this that I traverse the mountains covered with eternal snow. It is for this that I pass over the sandy plains in heat of summer, thirsting, and go for days without eating. But I shall count all this pleasure if I am at last allowed, by the all-wise God, the privilege of joining my family, and my friends.

Again the trappers decided to spend the winter with the Crow Indians in Wind River Valley. On December 24, 1829, snow had drifted around the buffalo skin lodges, and trees in the river bottom snapped with frost. A small fire burned in Jed's tepee, making it snug and warm. Furs, traps, tools, Bible, and account book were within easy reach.

Picking up the Bible, Jed turned to the second chapter of Luke and read the Christmas story. He remembered the happy Christmases in Ohio. His family always celebrated Christ's birth by reading the story of the angels' song, the manger, shepherds, wisemen, and the brightly shining star. The miracle of Bethlehem had hovered over them in their fun and games around a warm fire with bowls of popcorn, roasting chestnuts, and molasses taffy.

Jed held his mother's lock of hair in his hand, unconsciously rubbing it slowly between his fingers as he read. Abruptly he stopped at Mary's words to the young boy Jesus in the temple, "Son, why hast thou done this to us? Behold, thy father and I have sought thee sorrowing."

Did his mother feel this way about him, as Mary had felt about her Son?

A feeling of guilt swept over him, and a deep longing for his family filled him.

To his parents he wrote:

Your unworthy son once more undertakes to write his slighted parents. I have several times written but have received no answer from any of you since I left home, with the exception of Peter and Austin. The greatest pleasure I could enjoy would be to be in your company. I feel the need of the Christian church. You may well suppose that our society is the strangest kind. Men of good morals seldom enter this kind of business. I hope you will remember me before the Throne of Grace. May God in His infinite mercy allow me soon to join my parents, is the prayer of your undutiful son Jedediah.

As Jed thought about his family during those quiet winter evenings when he sat around the fire reading his Bible and writing in his journals, his mind wandered to many things. He had seen his dream fulfilled: He had explored and opened up the vast country between the Colorado and Columbia rivers, and it was but a matter of time before it would become a part of the United States. He had become quite wealthy and he wanted to share his money with his family and friends. That's what money was for, wasn't it—to share with people he loved?

In one of his letters to Ralph he said he would send money to Ralph to help educate his young brothers Benjamin and Nelson. Peter and Austin were already nineteen and twenty-one; they could take care of themselves. Jed confessed to being homesick and was thinking of quitting the trapping business, he added.

As the long winter came to an end, the trappers got busy. Davey Jackson took one group across the Rockies while Jed and his men moved north along the Musselshell River; the Blackfeet hovered around camp but did not attack. Jed was grateful to God for a safe trapping season.

In another letter Jed wrote Ralph that year, he said:

Are we grateful to that God in whom we live and move and have our being? How often we on bended knees offer our gratefulness for the gift of His dear Son! Is it possible that 'God so loved the world that He gave His only begotten Son that whosoever believeth in Him shall not perish but have everlasting life'? Then let us come forward with faith, nothing doubting, and He will unquestionably hear us—take my word for it, we shall be a blessing. Some, who have made a profession of

144

Christianity and have by their own negligence caused the Spirit to depart, think their day of grace is over. I find our Savior ever entreating and wooing us, using the most endearing language and endeavoring by every means without compelling, to bring us to him that we may have life. Are we doing our duty? Do we regularly attend to prayers and keep in mind that in due season we shall receive the crown if we faint not?

The trapping season passed quickly, and soon it was time for the rendezvous at Wind River. Excitement ran high that summer of 1830. Had the freight wagons made it safely across the mountains from the prairies to the east?

One day as Jed and Davey strained their eyes, ten heavily loaded freight wagons were slowly rolling overland from the east.

"Look! There they come!" shouted Davey.

This unusual caravan, with Billy Sublette in charge, had snaked across the virgin prairies of what is now Kansas and wound slowly up the Platte in western Nebraska, traveling a large part of what would become the Oregon Trail. They arrived at Wind River on Friday, July 16, 1830, behind them a cow and four steers surviving the long trek on foot.

The sound of gunfire, shrill whistles, and loud cheers greeted the wagons as they drew to a stop. The annual rendezvous had begun.

At this time Jed and his partners decided to sell out their trapping business to five men who wanted to take up where they had left off. It would now be called the Rocky Mountain Fur Company. Jed had had enough of the wilderness and was ready once again for civilization.

It was with great sorrow then that Jed read the message one of his brothers had sent by mail, which the freight wagons had delivered. His mother, Sally Strong Smith, had died. Jed had seen much death in his eight years on the trail, even of close friends. But never had it come so near, now that it had taken his mother.

"Jesus! the name that charms our fears,

That bids our sorrows cease;
'Tis music in the sinner's ears,
'Tis life, and health, and peace.
"He speaks, and, listening to His voice,
New life the dead receive,
The mournful, broken hearts rejoice,
The humble poor believe."

Tears burned Jed's eyes as the familiar hymn came to mind.

He folded the letter back up and put it in its envelope. Swinging his possibles bag from his shoulder, he took his Bible out. He placed the letter between its pages, next to her lock of hair. He touched the lock, then placed it in the envelope with the letter. For a moment he fingered his possibles bag (it was no longer the bright blue it had once been) and then slipped the Bible back into it.

Yes, it was time to leave the wilderness, with its wild mountains, parching deserts, and fierce Indians . . . at least for a time, perhaps forever.

Jedediah Smith would be nearer home now: He was headed back to St. Louis.

24

Good-bye, Shining Mountains

On August 4, 1830, the ten freight wagons, loaded with the furs of Jed and his partners, slowly began to roll eastward.

With the cheering farewell of the trappers who stayed behind ringing in his ears, Jed set his face toward the distant prairies. His work was done; he was eager to get home. He rode ahead on his horse as usual, his keen blue eyes on the dim, rutted trail ahead. Every once in a while he would turn in his saddle and look back at the mountains. Finally the Rockies' sharp, craggy outlines faded into a haze.

He was leaving the Shining Mountains behind, turning his back on the scenes of his fortunes and failures.

By September 10, the caravan had crawled across the prairies and reached the Blue River, stopping to rest at Pawnee villages in northeast Kansas Territory.

Sometimes Jed rode in the wagons, singing as he slapped the reins of the team, for it seemed he had spent a lifetime on horseback or on foot. It was good to be seated in a wagon and manage a team.

"You sure sound happy," Davey called out. "You haven't had your fill of adventurin' now, have you?"

Jed grinned. "Right now, I'm downright homesick. Sometimes I hope I never see a beaver again!"

Jed and Davey, each with a wagon, eager to reach home, pushed ahead of the others. They arrived in St. Louis the first week in October; the rest of the wagons rolled into the city on October 10, bringing in the greatest fortune in peltries ever to come down the Rockies.

The young Jedediah Strong Smith who had come so hopefully to St. Louis from the East eight years before was still a young man. But now he was coming from the West, from the mountains, and it showed. Neither his body nor his character had been broken, but rather strengthened.

When they rode slowly down the bustling streets, Jed was amazed. How St. Louis had grown! Besides Main Street between Walnut and Market being paved, the east-west streets, such as Olive and Chestnut, had been paved. The Catholics had finished their college with a new brick cathedral; on the corner of Fourth and St. Charles stood the new First Presbyterian Church; and at Third and Chestnut the Episcopalians had built Christ Church. There were new brickyards, quarries, and lumberyards—plus an iron foundry that made plows!

In the eager, waiting crowds that thronged the streets he spotted two familiar faces.

"Peter . . . Austin!" he cried, jumping from the wagon and running toward his brothers. They stared for a moment at the scarred, leather-tan features: the long, thin face, the ragged scar, the question-mark eyebrow, his body lean and muscled. The blue bandanna on his head partly covered his sun-bleached hair.

"Brother? Is it really you?" Austin cried.

"Yes, it's me!"

"Are you a mountain man . . . or a pirate?"

Jed laughed and hugged his brothers.

"Didn't you get our letters?" The two brothers hung onto their older brother eagerly.

Jed smiled wryly. Yes, he had received the letter from Peter and Austin, telling of their plans to strike out for the West themselves.

"We want to get rich like you, Jed." Austin's young face shone with dreams.

Jed understood their yearning for adventure only too well. But he also knew the dangers that lurked in the shadows

148

of the mountains, the blinding sands of the Salt Plains, the stark rugged trails in Oregon Country. Little had he known what rugged experiences he would face when he joined Major Ashley's trapping party. He had been so set on going West that he had tossed all caution to the winds because he wanted to "fill the empty spaces" on the map. He wasn't ready to allow his brothers to rush brashly into the unknown, as he had.

"We'll talk about it later," he said with a quiet smile.

The next day the editor of the *St. Louis Beacon* published a story about Jed Smith and Davey Jackson in the newspaper.

> We understand that these gentlemen have done well; that they bring in a large amount of furs, and are richly rewarded for their perils and enterprise. Mr. Smith has been out eight years, and has explored the country from the Gulf of California to the south of the Columbia. We hope to be able to give a more particular account of the extraordinary enterprises of these gentlemen, and the country they have explored.

Jed wasn't too interested in what the paper had to say; he was busy doing some of the things that had filled his mind lately. After he had sold the furs and paid his men, he arranged for his youngest brothers, Benjamin and Nelson, to go to school. Then he bought a table service to send to Ralph's wife, Louisa, daughter of Dr. Simons. They had been friends for so long. He also sent money to his father and Dr. Simons and presented two thousand dollars to the Methodist Church.

When the church bells rang on Sunday morning, Jed Smith was there. It was so good to be back "in the watch and care of the church." His fellowship with Christians had been infrequent.

Jed made a trip to Ashtabula to visit his family and good friend Dr. Simons. He stood silently for a long moment at his mother's grave. He wished she knew that he had invested a part of his money in a farm and even a town house in St. Louis, that he had plans to settle down.

When he went back to St. Louis, he began to arrange his notes, filling in the blank spaces in his memory as best as he could, for some records had been lost. Writing a book took much skill and know-how, he discovered.

One day he met Samual Parkman, a friend of the family who had become well-educated.

"I'm working on a book of my experiences," Jed told him, "but my punctuation and grammar and spelling is terrible. Sammy, I need your help to put my manuscript together right."

"I'll do what I can to help," Parkman told him.

Jed also began a large new map, which included more accurate routes and trails than previous maps, adding sites and names of Indian tribes as well.

While working on his manuscript he could not fail to hear the business talk of the town: the Santa Fe trade. So when his former partners proposed a business venture there, he listened. One day he also entertained a visitor from Connecticut.

"My name is Jonathan Trumbull Warner," the young man introduced himself. "I've been very sick and came out here to get well. I want to be a trapper. Isn't it true that trappers have many adventures, and that buffalo meat is better than any medicine?"

Jed tried to stifle a chuckle. "Look, young man," he said, his voice firm, "if you go to the mountains your chances of meeting death are much greater than getting well." Jed pointed to the scar over his eyebrow and then pulled back his hair to reveal the ear that had been sewn back.

The young man grimaced, as if feeling the pain for himself.

"And if you should survive the terrible ordeal in the wilderness and regain your health," his gaze swung away from his listener to fix itself on the distant western skyline, "you won't be much good for anything else . . ." He looked back at Warner. "Take my advice and stay out of the mountains.

It's obvious from your speech and your appearance that you're an educated man. You can do something better with your life rather than risk it as a trapper."

The young man took Jed's advice and bided his time. Very shortly he did go West, not as a trapper but as a clerk—on Jed's business venture to Santa Fe. There he would join Davey Jackson's party to San Diego, eventually using his education to become an influencial and well-known man in the Province of California, adopting Mexican citizenship and the name Jose Juan Warner.

One day while Jed and his partners were working on the book and maps, a reporter came to Jed's home.

"I'd like to talk to you," he told Jed.

"I'm sorry, but there's really not much to tell," he said with a shrug of his shoulders. "Besides, I've much work to do on my book."

Billy Sublette shouldered his way toward the reporter. "If Jed won't talk, let me give you the facts about"—here he cleared his throat—"Jedediah Strong Smith."

As Billy talked, the reporter furiously jotted down notes.

"I understand that Mr. Smith was the first American to make his way to California from the East and cross the Sierra Nevada Mountains. He is also said to be the first white man to cross the Great Salt Lake Desert." The reported paused. "Now that makes good copy. But will people believe the other things you've told me about him? About being a Christian gentleman? How can a leader of rough mountain men—"

"Jed Smith is that, all right," Billy interrupted. "He never takes a drink or uses bad language. In the mountains he broke holes in the ice to get water to shave. He has been clean-shaven all the years that I've known him. Each night he reads his Bible and often sang hymns as he rode through the wilderness. He is gentle, but he can lick any trapper who breaks his rules."

The reporter's eyes narrowed. "Nobody'll believe that," he scoffed.

"I was there, *friend*," said Billy.

At the word "friend," the reporter took a step back.

"H-How can a man be tough and gentle both?"

"Easy," growled Billy. "Just be like Jedediah Strong Smith—half preacher and half grizzly!"

"And reckon the Christian life as 'the one thing needful,' " put in Davey Jackson, "like Jed says. Now, can you argue with that?"

The reporter grabbed his notes and scurried off without another word.

Billy Sublette and Davey Jackson had been toying with the idea of taking a caravan of goods down the Santa Fe Trail to New Mexico to trade and were working on plans. Jed finally decided to invest some of his funds in this venture.

Late in December Jed's brother Ira arrived in St. Louis to try to sell some hand type.

"No printer seems to want it, Jed." He looked at the floor.

Jed threw his arm over his brother's shoulder and took him outside. Pointing to St. Louis College, he said, "See those buildings over there?"

"Yes, sir."

"You belong there—or least some place similar. Ira, you're young. If you'd get an education you could make something of yourself, instead of piddling around."

Not long afterwards, Jed took Ira to Jacksonville, Illinois, and enrolled him in college.

But Peter and Austin were still pestering Jed to let them go West. "You had your chance at adventure. Why can't we?"

Jed shook his head. "Sorry, boys. . . . But I tell you what: My partners plan to take goods to Santa Fe by freight wagon, and I expect to invest in the project. Would an expedition to Santa Fe do?" *At least there'll be no mountains or salt flats to cross,* he thought to himself.

Peter and Austin looked at each other and grinned. "When do we leave?" they chorused.

25

Jed's Last Adventure

For some four years freight wagons had made the long trek from Independence, Missouri, the westernmost settlement on the Missouri River, to Santa Fe, New Mexico. At this outpost of the Southwest, goods were exchanged or sold for materials from Mexico.

At first Jed hadn't planned to make the trip with Peter and Austin. He figured if his partners captained the train, his brothers were in good hands.

"What do you think, Davey? Austin's peddled Yankee notions on the road from Pennsylvania to Ohio, and Peter's taken a wagon of goods—clocks and medicines and such like—from Ashtabula down into Illinois."

"Jed," Davey spit and wiped his mouth, "compared to your mountain and desert routes, this trail we're taking to Santa Fe is a picnic."

"I don't know, Davey. They're on the young side."

"Around here it's the thing for young fellers to take a trip to Santa Fe before settling down," Davey reminded Jed. "Sure, there's maybe some Indians along the trail, but we're not worried. We're a strong bunch and we're taking plenty of arms to protect ourselves. We're even taking Big Betsy, the cannon."

Later in February, however, Jed changed his mind about not going. "I'll go along far enough to get you boys started, then I'll come back."

He gathered his papers and other personal property, boxed

153

them up, and took them to General Ashley for safekeeping. Among the articles he wanted to keep were his book manuscript, some grizzly bear skins, sea otter pelts, his bow and arrows, rifle and guns, saddle, and private papers.

When word came from a wandering trapper that the Blackfeet Indians, far from their usual hunting grounds, had been seen among swarms of hostile Indians along the Santa Fe Trail, Jed grew uneasy. He'd never trusted the Blackfeet.

I don't want my brothers to face those Indians without me, he thought. *I'd better go all the way to Santa Fe with them.* Besides, he told his old partners as they smirked at each other, "For all my travel in the Southwest, I've not laid eyes on Santa Fe." Perhaps adventure still sang in his blood, after all.

Sammy Parkman was with Jed when he made up his mind to go. With thoughts of his family still on his mind, Jed dictated his will and testament to his friend, just to be safe. It was a simple document: His father was to receive two hundred dollars a year from Jed's estate; the rest was to be divided among his brothers and sisters, Ralph, Austin, Peter, Ira, Benjamin, Nelson, Sally Jones, Betsy Davis, and Eunice Simons. The young man from Connecticut, Jonathan Warner, witnessed the will.

On April 10, 1831, a caravan of twenty-two loaded wagons headed up the Missouri River valley.

The party spent several days at Independence, adding stores to their freight, including needles, thread, ribbon, cotton and woolen cloth, shawls, crepes, silks, velvets, and a variety of other goods not available in New Mexico.

Besides Smith, Jackson, and Sublette, the Irishman Thomas Fitzpatrick, bound for St. Louis and supplies, joined the caravan; indeed, among the eighty-seven men who made up the final party, a large number were seasoned mountain men. There were a few greenhorns, like Austin and Peter, as well as a handful of sportsmen and adventurers.

Jed, always preferring to be clean-shaven, took along a dressing case that held a mirror, razors, and soap.

The group left on May 4, 1831.

At Council Grove in Kansas Territory they made final preparations at the Last Chance store and picked up the latest word about the long trail ahead. Here Jed saw the spreading oak tree called Council Oak, the site of an Indian peace treaty. He hoped it meant that the Kaws, Osages, Kiowas, and Cheyennes were peaceful now.

Even though the Santa Fe was a well-defined route by now, travelers sometimes took shortcuts. But the wind, shifting sand, and buffalo tracks often erased these cutoffs and the wagons were forced to make new ones. For the first 350 miles the landmarks were plain, and nothing unusual happened. Then the party reached the Arkansas River in southwest Kansas, near the present site of Dodge City. They were just over halfway in their journey. Here a young man named Minter went off chasing antelope and a band of Pawnees killed him. It was a bad sign.

Here, rather than taking the longer but safer route along the Arkansas, they decided to go directly for the Cimarron River. Now they began the hardest part of the journey.

South of the Arkansas where the Cimarron cuts across northwest Oklahoma near what is now the Panhandle, a flat barren plain stretched unbroken for some sixty miles. For anyone taking a shortcut, the usual landmarks were missing. One writer of the period called it "the grand prairie ocean . . . all is as level as the sea."

"When we find water we'd better lay in a good supply," Jed cautioned. "It could be scarce along the way."

The landscape may have been like an ocean of grass, but it held no watering hole. Day after day hot winds whipped across the prairies. But like Davey Jackson had said, Jed had crossed much worse routes.

"You'll find a water hole this side of the Cimarron," they were told at the last stopping place. "You can't miss it."

As the freight wagons angled off on the shortcut, they found the spring without trouble—It was dry and choked with sand.

In their disappointment the travelers followed a buffalo

155

trail, deciding that animals usually knew where to find water. Yet mile after mile of barren plains produced nothing but dry creeks. As a matter of fact, a drought that spring would make the year go down as one of the driest in history. Men scattered in all directions looking for water, without any luck.

On Friday morning, May 27, the third day of their search for water, Jed mounted his horse again. Tom Fitzpatrick did the same.

The two men rode out across the plains in heat that already shimmered like a wall in whatever direction they looked.

At mid-morning they reined in their horses at a dry stream bed. "I don't think my horse can go much farther, Jed. I believe I'll dig here til I find a little something for him."

Jed gazed at the shimmering horizon. "You do that. I'll just go ahead a ways . . . along this buffalo path. Maybe the Cimarron is just over that rise."

Jed rode southwest. For a moment horse and rider stood on top of a low knoll, silhouetted against the glaring blue sky, then disappeared. No white man ever saw the great pathfinder, the buckskinned grizzly-fighter, the "Bibletotin'" mountaineer, again.

Alone, Jed rode on in his search for water. Now mirage after mirage mocked him, drawing him on just a little farther. Finally, having dismounted, he led his horse into the dry wash of a stream and stumbled down toward the parched bed of the Cimarron.

Suddenly Jed squinted his eyes. Didn't that spot in the riverbed look damp? He pulled his horse after him. Reaching the spot, he dropped to his knees and scooped a hole in the sand. As water seeped into it, he cupped his hands and drank. Then digging a little more and moving aside, he drew his horse to the spot. As he did so, he noticed a sight that caused him to slowly mount his horse while it drank: Just beyond the bank, a dozen Indians were peering at him— Comanche—some of the boldest and most warlike Indians of the plains.

Jed realized he couldn't fight all of them. The only thing left was to show them he was their friend. As he had done so often before, he clasped his hands in front of him with the usual peace sign. They ignored his friendly gestures.

Two of the Indians shook blankets at his horse as another flashed sunlight from a hand mirror into its eyes. The animal reared and spun around.

At that moment a long Comanche lance, attached to a hair rope, streaked through the air and pierced Jed's body. He whirled his horse back around and fired his rifle. The ball struck and killed the chief. But the rest rushed upon Jed with arrows, lances, and knives. Jed drew his pistol and fired again.

Jedediah Strong Smith died on Friday, May 27, 1831, a month shy of his thirty-third birthday. How exactly he died would never be learned, for his body was never found and only second- and third-hand stories relayed the tale.

To his brother Austin fell the grim task of notifying the family. He wrote to Ralph:

> It is my painful duty to communicate to you the death of our lamented brother Jedediah. He was killed by the Comanche Indians . . . on the Cimarron River between Arkansas River and Santa Fe. His company and Sublette's consisting of 74 men, and animals for 22 wagons, was on the point of starving for want of water (near four days without any). . . . He saw the Indians before they attacked. . . . He therefore went boldly up with the hope of making peace with them, but found that [his] only chance was defense. . . . I have his gun and pistols, got from the Indians by the traders.

> Such, my dear brother, is the fate of our guardian and protector on this route; him, who had gone through so many dangers, so many privations; and almost at the time when he had reached the goal of his enterprise, to be thus torn from us is lamentable indeed. But let us not grieve too much, for he trusted in a wise and a powerful Being.

And so, abruptly closed the colorful life of Jedediah Smith in whose blood sang adventure but whose soul trusted in God. It is said of Jedediah Smith that "he made the lone wilderness a place of meditation, the mountaintop his altar."

Jed had finished his last adventure in his concern for his family. Now his restless moccasins were stilled, the great map unfinished. But the South Pass, across the Great Divide, would open up passage for civilization, for more traders, pioneers, homesteaders. Beyond the Shining Mountains, his treks to the Pacific—across two formidable deserts and a mountain chain—had brought back word of an inviting land, a land that had to be seen to be believed.

But more than leaving word of what lay west, Jedediah Strong Smith left a legacy of character. He was faithful to God and to family. More than a doer of great exploits, he was a man of Christian character—*God's* mountain man.

For Further Reading

Burt, Olive W. *Jedediah Smith, Fur Trapper of the Old West.* London: Julian Messner, Inc., Publishers, 1951.

————. *Young Jed Smith: Westering Boy.* New York: The Bobbs-Merrill Co., Inc., 1954.

Evarts, Hal George. *Jedediah Smith, Trail Blazer of the West.* New York: Putnam Publishing Group, 1958.

Johnson, Jalman. *Builders of the Northwest.* Toronto: Dodd, Mead & Co., 1963.

Latham, Frank. *Jed Smith.* New York: Aladdin Books, 1952.

Miller, Helen M. *Jed Smith and the Far Frontier.* New York: Putnam Publishing Group, 1971.

Neihardt, John. *The Splendid Wayfaring.* New York: Macmillan Publishing Co., Inc., 1920; reprint Lincoln, Nebr.: University Press, 1970.

Smith, Alson. *Men Against the Mountains.* Athens, Ohio: J. H. Day Publishing Co., 1965.

Sullivan, Maurice S. *Jedediah Smith: Trader and Trailblazer.* New York: Press of the Pioneers, Inc., 1936.